Famous Scots and the Supernatural

Famous Scots and the Supernatural

Ron Halliday

BLACK & WHITE PUBLISHING

First published 2012
by Black & White Publishing Ltd
29 Ocean Drive, Edinburgh EH6 6JL

1 3 5 7 9 10 8 6 4 2   12 13 14 15

ISBN: 978 1 84502 457 4

The publisher has made every reasonable effort to contact copyright holders of images in the picture section. Any errors are inadvertent and anyone who for any reason has not been contacted is invited to write to the publisher so that a full acknowledgment can be made in subsequent editions of this work.

A CIP catalogue record for this book is available from the British Library.

Typeset by Ellipsis Digital Ltd, Glasgow
Printed and bound by MPG Books Ltd, Bodmin

Contents

An Introduction to Famous Scots and the Supernatural

Ever since I was given a copy of the traditional tales of King Arthur and the Knights of the Round Table as a child I have been fascinated by the myths and legends linked to this mystical figure. John Boorman's 1981 film *Excalibur* remains my favourite picture, and I've often wondered why Arthur's name resonates down the centuries. I suspect that a large part of the answer lies in the way that he moves from one world to another, from the land of everyday reality to the country of enchantment, and draws back the veil which allows us to peer into the unseen, a place populated by all sorts of phantoms and strange entities. Our world of today may be vastly different from that inhabited by Arthur, but in many ways the same threads run through it. What is out there? Do the spirits of the dead live on? Are there individuals possessed with mystical powers? Can unseen entities – ghosts, nature spirits, and a host of other forms – be contacted? If so, Scotland seems the place to do it.

Over the years, I have been involved with several of the many mediums and psychics our country has produced and have had some astonishing results. One such project had a direct impact on this book and is recounted in chapter seven.

However, while engaged in investigation, I became intrigued by another aspect of the paranormal, one usually ignored: What effect has the supernatural had on the lives and careers of famous Scots? Over the years I gathered bits of information relating to some well-known figures and their interests in the paranormal, many of whom surprised me. Eventually, I decided that a full-blown investigation might be rewarding. I was, however, astonished by what I found. It significantly altered my view of some of the most famous figures in our history. Far from being a sideshow, the supernatural played a key role in the lives of many of the best-known Scots, including those with worldwide reputations.

In fact, all the individuals covered in *Famous Scots and the Supernatural* have played a significant part in the fields in which they were active, either as writers, artists, politicians, scientists or military men. Some, like William Wallace or Robert the Bruce, are national heroes. Others, such as Ramsay MacDonald, have enjoyed a less favourable press, even though they are important figures in historical terms. To include them in this book, however, I had to be sure that the supernatural in some form or another had played an influential part in shaping each individual's career or life, particularly where some significant act was involved. Donald Dewar and the construction of the Scottish Parliament is a fascinating example, as is the role of the supernatural in John Logie Baird's invention of television.

Certain people were obsessed with the supernatural and here I can cite the case of James Hogg for whom the world beyond influenced him from the day of his birth. Other figures, such as Hugh Dowding, found themselves interacting with the paranormal almost by chance, but having been drawn into its spell, were no less intense on the subject than those who had imbibed it from birth.

What can we learn from the experience of the famous? That James VI believed in the reality of witchcraft doesn't prove that the Devil exists and is trying to take over the world! In short, *Famous Scots and the Supernatural* is not about proving that ghosts, phantoms or spirit beings are real; however, what I hope it does show is that no matter how talented or able a person may be, a belief in the existence of the paranormal can exert a powerful influence on the mind and so affect the way an individual behaves in whatever field he or she may be active. One can go deeper than that, though, because the individuals I have written about have played an important part in history so that the supernatural, through the lives of the famous, has impacted on the lives of many people, even whole nations. If William Wallace had not been seen as a leader with the supernatural world on his side would he have been as successful in rallying Scotland against Edward I during the Wars of Independence? Without encouragement from the spirit world would John Logie Baird have invented television? Or Douglas Haig so determinedly have pressed the fight against Germany in World War I? These are fascinating questions for which I hope I have provided if not answers that everyone will agree on, at least food for thought and a fresh insight on the motivation of those covered in this book.

Historians generally have little interest in the part played by the paranormal in world events. This I will admit is not a cast-iron principle; Gary Mead in his biography of Douglas Haig makes reference to the Haig family's interest in Spiritualism, and David Marquand in writing about Ramsay MacDonald includes material relating to the Prime Minister's involvement in the subject, but I would suggest that these are the exceptions to the general rule that the supernatural is overlooked or downplayed where the lives of the famous are concerned, as virtually no books have it as a focus or key theme. However, as I hope I demonstrate, by excluding the effect of the supernatural on the lives of key historical figures writers ignore what can form a significant aspect of what drives the famous to achievement and influences decision making. The supernatural as a factor in an individual's life deserves, where the evidence exists, to occupy a role more centre stage. Without giving the other world in the careers of the famous the attention it merits we don't get a full picture of that individual and so end up with a distorted view of their lives. I certainly found that in researching this book many of those I looked at turned out to be far more complex figures than I had at first imagined! I hope that after reading *Famous Scots and the Supernatural* you will be as surprised as I was about the mystical interests of some of our best-known figures.

It may also surprise readers to discover that interest in the supernatural is not confined to one era of Scottish history. I've no doubt that the period of the witchcraft trials in the sixteenth and seventeenth centuries stands out as a time when the paranormal most obviously impacted on well-known individuals – James VI and Mary Queen of Scots, for example – and historical events. But that was only the most dramatic event in a long line of interactions between key figures and the paranormal. In less obvious but equally bizarre ways, the world beyond has impacted succeeding generations of Scots, from St Mungo in the sixth century to Donald Dewar in the twentieth, and every period in between and after.

In Scotland at least, the supernatural has played a role, in a variety of ways, in influencing the thoughts and acts of those with the talent to rise to the top in their area of activity. In writing *Famous Scots and the Supernatural* I should explain that, as the book focuses on individuals from diverse backgrounds and different historical periods, I set out to place each person in the context of the time in which they lived and give an account of his or her career. By doing so I hope I have succeeded in each case in explaining exactly how and the extent to which the supernatural played a role in their lives.

No book can be written without the efforts of those who have gone before. Given the well-known faces that I have written about the total literature is vast and I have selected only those which have had the most direct relevance to the subject covered in *Famous Scots and the Paranormal*. The number of books published on the Jacobites and Bonnie Prince Charlie, for example, is so extensive it would fill a bibliography on its own! A few individuals, however, have had surprisingly little coverage. Donald Dewar is an example of a key Scottish figure about whom little has so far been written. In researching for this book I was fortunate that we possess in central Scotland several libraries with extensive book and historical document collections. I've made use of the National Library of Scotland for more years than I care to think about! But the Scottish library in Edinburgh Central Library has a fantastic set of books, as has Glasgow's Mitchell Library and so-handy-for-me Stirling University Library. My sincere thanks to all these institutions and their staff.

Over the years since I started investigating the paranormal, I have been lucky to receive the help of many colleagues. I'd mention the work I did with Malcolm Robinson some years back and more recently the assistance on several projects of medium Gary Gray. It goes without saying that my parents – inadvertently I'm sure! – had a big impact in propelling me down the path of psychic investigation. So thanks to Ron and Mary Halliday for that.

I'd like once again to thank Black & White Publishing for their continued interest in books on the paranormal and for taking *Famous Scots and the Supernatural* on board. I must thank all the staff at Black & White, but particularly Alison McBride, and also Kristen Susienka for her editorial assistance.

Finally, I would like to thank my wife Evelyn for reading over each chapter and for her suggestions on the content. I would also like to express my thanks for her constant support and for tolerating the substantial amount of time over many months I spent on *Famous Scots and the Supernatural*. Finishing it all was a great relief for her!

Ron Halliday, Bridge of Allan

1

The Early Mystics and
the Rise of the Supernatural

Why do the words 'Scotland' and 'supernatural' seem to run so easily together? Was it always this way? Maybe so, but it is certainly possible to establish a time when the paranormal first impacted on our history, and the people who played the major part in bringing this about.

It is said that three people created the image of Scotland as a land of enchantment where the world of reality and the supernatural collide: St Columba, St Kentigern and Arthur. In all three cases the paranormal played an important part in influencing their actions, and they in turn established forever the sense that Scotland was a land where the veil to other worlds could be lifted more easily than elsewhere. From then on, like the ripples from a stone thrown into the water, the supernatural's influence spread out to embrace every part of society. By the time of William Wallace and the Wars of Independence, the supernatural had become a force that everyone took seriously and wanted to have on their side.

King Arthur

In January 2012 a story broke in the media that King Arthur's grave had been discovered at a site near Selkirk in the Scottish Borders. It was claimed that his body lay beneath the Yarrow Stone, an ancient, time worn monolith. The marker had, in fact, been discovered several hundred years earlier, but a review by experts of the inscription carved on the headstone suggested a reference to the legendary King, a fact that had not been realised before. The revelation made worldwide headlines. Whether or not Arthur's body was at one time entombed at this location will probably never be known for sure, but what is extraordinary about this story is the excitement his name generates even today. Fifteen hundred years after his death, King Arthur resonates in a way that few people from history, no matter how well known, can match.

But was there a real King Arthur? Or is he no more than a figment of someone's poetic imagination? Or a bit of both? Did he originate in Wales, England or Scotland? Traditionally, he has been linked to sites in Cornwall, at Tintagel and Cadbury Castle in Somerset, which is said to be the Camelot of legend. In fact, many places in the south and south west of England, and even as far north as Shropshire, have claimed Arthur as their own. In recent years, however, there has been a move to question a southern connection for the king, as this link was based on accounts by English medieval historians anxious to glorify their past. A growing consensus now emerging is that the legends of Arthur are based on a real person and more and more his activities are being linked to Scotland's ancient history.

So what of the real Arthur? We know that the first reference to him was in a poem 'Y Gododdin' composed in about 600 AD

King Arthur

which celebrated the war heroes of the tribe that ruled the lands south of the Firth of Forth. He could, in all probability, have been the chief or war leader of these people. It is also said that Arthur stood and watched a battle between his forces and the Picts from the hill near the centre of Edinburgh, which still bears his name, Arthur's Seat. And there are many other claimed connections with Scotland.

An ancient coffin, carved out of a single block of solid stone and discovered in Govan Old Parish Church in 1885, is said to have once contained the body of King Arthur. The stone is marked with an 'A' and has not been engraved with any Christian symbols. It also seems to be decorated with the insignia of a Celtic-style warrior. Although it is not possible to prove that this is Arthur's resting place, it demonstrates the long-standing tradition of a link between Arthur and lowland Scotland.

Nearby at Dumbarton rock we have another 'Arthur's Seat' and the site itself has been linked to King Rhydderch Hael, whose wife Langoureth the Christian saint Kentigern allegedly saved from being put to death. She was also, by tradition, the sister of Merlin the magician. A curious link between history, legend and the supernatural. Near Falkirk can be found Arthur's Oe'n, or Arthur's Oven, so named for its circular shape and said to be the site of the legendary Round Table. The building no longer exists, but the drawings that survive suggest it was neither old enough nor large enough to be the centre for the court of a king of Arthur's stature. But in the same area is the district of Camelon which excites interest because it is situated in the geographical location where Arthur may have been active and its name sounds similar to Camlann, Arthur's last battle and the one in which he was mortally wounded.

From the battlefield Arthur was transported to the Isle

of Avalon which, it has been argued, could be the island of Arran. Or so tradition has it. In *Arthur and the Lost Kingdoms*, Alistair Moffat has made a strong case for Arthur having been active in the Borderlands with a base at the now defunct city of Roxburgh. So Camelot itself could have been located in Scotland. However, it is to be doubted whether the case will be proved one way or the other, though a Scottish connection for the legendary king seems to be well supported by the available evidence.

But one fact seems beyond doubt. If a king was ever linked to the power of other worlds, it is Arthur. He was, by tradition, brought into the world thanks to the magic of the sorcerer Merlin who shape-shifted Uther Pendragon so that Igraine, the wife of the Duke of Cornwall, was tricked into believing he was her husband and slept with him. Arthur was the result of this union of mystical forces. The baby was taken by Merlin, who brought him up in obscurity. The supernatural emerged again to raise Arthur to the kingship when he famously drew the sword from the stone to prove his right to the throne. He was also given a magical weapon, Excalibur, by the mystical Lady of the Lake. The fact is that a host of stories involving the supernatural have attached themselves to Arthur. But why should that have happened?

Arthur lived at a time after the collapse of the Roman Empire when various tribes were battling for control of Scotland. He has been pictured as leader of the Britons, the ancient peoples of that name, fighting to defend his land against invading Angles, Saxons, Scots and Picts. At the same time, Christianity was replacing pagan religions, such as Druidism, but this too involved a struggle though of wills rather than swords. Later writers depicted Arthur as a Christian warrior, even describing the symbol of the Virgin Mary he carried on his shield into battle. Why on earth then is he so closely linked to Merlin, an obvious representative of the old beliefs and quite clearly no Christian? Merlin is even described in Christian literature as a key opponent of St Kentigern, one of the first Christian missionaries of the sixth century, in the struggle between the old and new religions. The association between Arthur and Merlin is an enigma, if Arthur truly was the Christian warrior later tradition made him out to be.

Throughout Scottish history leaders were constantly compared to Arthur, in terms of their ability as warriors and leaders. His reputation was enormous. But he was also seen as a figure who inhabited a magical realm. In 1568 William Stewart and Sir Archibald Napier, who were on trial for sorcery, were accused of having attempted to conjure the spirit of the king, appropriately on Edinburgh's Arthur's Seat. And an arrested witch, Janet Boyman, was alleged to have done the same and addressed the spirit she raised in the name 'of the Father and Son, of Elspeth, Queen of the Fairies and of King Arthur'. Most of the sites which bear his name, including Loch Arthur in Kirkcudbright and Ben Arthur – often called The Cobbler – in Argyll, are geographical locations which were important in pagan worship. Spots which facilitated contact with the spirits of the mystic lands.

It was also believed that Arthur and his knights lay asleep beneath the Eildon Hills in the Borders, waiting to be roused and come to Scotland's aid in time of war. Even as late as the Jacobite rising of 1745, the leader, Charles Edward Stuart, was compared to a new Arthur, come to cleanse the land of usurpers – the Hanoverian kings in this case. It's interesting to note, however, that there was a tinge of suspicion surrounding Arthur because of his supposed links to the south. King Edward I of England, to take one instance, was forever claiming to be the true descendent of the legendary king, boasting of his possession of Arthur's crown. Even so, Arthur maintained his Scottish status as a brave leader, being referred to as such by John Barbour, author of the fourteenth-century epic *The Bruce*, covering his hero's career, and also praised by the fifteenth-century poet known as Blind Harry as 'Good King Arthur' in his account of William Wallace's life that compares the two as warriors and leaders.

So who was the real Arthur? When we think of Arthur we automatically also conjure up an image of Merlin. The two men seem so closely linked that I sometimes wonder whether they are two aspects of the same individual. We have Arthur the war leader, rooted in reality, on the one hand. Whereas Merlin, on the other hand, could be the king in his shamanistic role, the wanderer among the enchanted lands. The combination of the real world and the realm of magic within one individual is a common theme of the ancient traditions. However, the legends that have come down to us suggest that we are dealing with distinct individuals who may, in fact, have even lived in different eras.

The true identity of these key figures may never be fully known; however, evidence of their influence in the world today continues to be acknowledged and appreciated, leaving no doubt that the heroes' legends are still very much alive in the world today.

St Kentigern

Genuine evidence from a past fifteen hundred years ago is hard to come by. But although there has never been a tradition that St Kentigern, an important founding father of Christianity in Scotland, met King Arthur, there are many accounts of his confrontation with Merlin. A stained-glass window in a church in the Borders village of Stobo depicts a meeting between the two.

Kentigern, sometimes known as Mungo, is the patron saint of Glasgow. He is a key figure in the growth of Christianity in Scotland in the sixth century, having, more or less, founded Glasgow as a centre of the new religion. But Kentigern was not a Christian in the way we would recognise today. He was more like a shamanistic figure, a sorcerer who wielded supernatural powers. He brought into Christianity the pagan idea that this world, the one we live in, interacted with the other world, and the one could influence the other. St Kentigern, in his life and actions, lived out this theme. He undoubtedly aimed at converting the pagan world to Christianity, but in doing this he was forced to adopt the ideas and behaviour of the ancient ways. It has had a permanent influence on the way that Scots picture themselves.

In fact, St Kentigern, who lived between 520 and 612 AD, appears to have more in common with the famous 'magician' Merlin than with the present day functions of a minister or priest. It could be argued that St Kentigern is linked with Merlin, as a bridge between different eras, the pagan and the Christian. St Kentigern possessed the sort of paranormal powers you'd only expect to find in a wizard or mystic. He brought a dead bird back to life. He made a frozen branch burst into flames. In Glasgow he made the ground rise to form a hill, known as Dovehill. He could make objects move through time and space.

The very circumstances of his birth were surrounded by otherworldly events, which marked him as a mystic. His mother, Enoch, was the daughter of a king of Lothian. She fell pregnant but, as she was not married, her father had her thrown from the top of Traprain Law. She was miraculously saved from death, but the king, her father, was determined to punish her. He set his daughter out on a boat alone on the Firth of Forth. But once again the supernatural intervened. A shoal of fish appeared which escorted her across the water till she landed safely in the village of Culross on the Fife coast. It was here that St Kentigern was born.

The arrival of the fish and their role in saving Enoch and her baby was not simply meant as a fanciful story. It was intended to convey the notion of supernatural intervention at the very start of Kentigern's life. But was this simply meant as a Christian link? Probably not, for though the fish symbol is linked to Christianity, it has a long association with age-old religions stretching back to ancient Egypt, where it was linked to the fertility gods, as well as the time of the druids when the Fisher King was also an important entity connected to the underworld, of which he was a protector.

Kentigern's association with Glasgow came as an adult. He was, in fact, brought up in Culross by Serf, a holy hermit. The manner in which he came to set up his Christian mission at the 'dear green place', which is the meaning of Glasgow, strikes one as simply bizarre. The pagan elements in what happened seem difficult to deny. So what on earth was going on? The description of the events was given by a monk known as Jocelyn, who wrote about St Kentigern in the twelfth century, several hundred years after his death. Whether reliance can be placed on his account of the life of the saint is in a way not relevant. He was happy to include a range of miracles associated with Kentigern and a host of odd events, as even in the period he wrote with Christianity well established, he clearly saw no harm in linking his hero to the type of activity we would view today as 'magical' or even downright pagan.

As a young man, Kentigern had become friendly with a hermit known as Fergus who lived in a sacred grove at St Ninian's near Stirling. On the death of Fergus, Kentigern yoked two untamed bulls to Fergus's funeral cart and transported the body 'by a straight road along which there was no path as far as Glasgow', as *The Life of St Kentigern*, Jocelyn's account, records it. The saint then buried Fergus in a cemetery consecrated by St Ninian, in which 'none other man had yet lain'. Although briefly described, this short account by Jocelyn raises a host of questions: Why did Kentigern use bulls for a journey of some thirty miles or more? What was the mysterious 'straight road' he followed? What was the significance of the spot he chose to bury Fergus? And was this more a pagan than Christian rite?

Bulls, or oxen, have little or no connection with the Christian religion. In fact, James Hastings' classic *Dictionary of the Bible*, originally published in 1909 and reprinted many times since, has virtually no reference to their significance, except as animals of sacrifice. But as a symbol for pagans they vied with horses in importance. The god Baal who does feature in the Bible as an enemy of the new religion, in one legend linked to him copulates with a heifer from which an ox is born who becomes Baal's twin brother. In Persian mythology, the god Ohrmazd created the primal bull, called Gosh, at the same moment as he created the first man. From the earliest period in the history of ancient Egypt the bull was worshipped as a symbol of strength and virility; it is known today as the cult of Apis. A sacred bull was chosen and kept in seclusion to be paraded on religious festivals. On its death it was embalmed and buried within an underground cemetery.

So why was Kentigern using animals linked to paganism to haul a Christian figure's funeral cart? It's certainly curious. And what was the strange 'straight road' that wasn't, in fact, a proper road that he was following? Once again we find ourselves dealing with a pagan concept. According to pre-Christian tradition, the earth was crossed by invisible streams of energy that travelled in a straight line. Many ancient monuments, particularly standing stone circles, were situated where these lines crossed. These paths of energy, called 'ley lines' by modern dowsers, were seen as special places which facilitated contact with other worlds. To travel along them was to follow a sacred path. Clearly, when Kentigern took Fergus' body to Glasgow he was travelling a ritual route, one that must have been pagan in origin. But equally strange is the claim that St Kentigern actually raised the cortege off the ground so that it floated along as if on invisible rails on its journey. Did St Kentigern tap into a mysterious force generated from below the ground? It's an odd aspect of a very strange story. And why did he choose that particular spot to bury Fergus? By tradition it stands close to the present site of Glasgow Cathedral, the place where Kentigern set up his first church. Long before the saint arrived, however, this area was viewed as a mystic location. It was sacred to the druids, and other pagan sects which time has long forgotten. St Kentigern brought Fergus' body to this spot and made it his base quite deliberately. For Kentigern too, its mystical aura clearly had a strong appeal. The interaction between our world and other magical realms was not a factor which at this time Christianity rejected. Kentigern was as willing as any druid or practitioner of magic to use the supernatural to overcome his enemies, those opposed to the new religion.

The feats he performed may or may not have happened. It all depends on your view of the power of magic. There's no denying though that they were symbolic of ideas and forces, the knowledge of which we have long forgotten. They may come across to us now as no more than strange, unfathomable tales, but the involvement of supernatural forces, whether actual or fanciful, is undeniable.

On one occasion there were no men to work in the fields,

so St Kentigern ordered two deer to yoke themselves to the plough, which they duly did. They continued to work the land till the day a wolf appeared and killed and ate one of the deer. St Kentigern then ordered the wolf to take the stag's place and it obeyed him. No doubt there are levels of meaning to this tale. It reveals St Kentigern's mystic character, a shaman-like individual. A man in tune with and having the ability to control the forces of nature. By speaking to and ruling over the wild beasts he became, in a sense, the spirit of that animal. The link to the practice of many ancient peoples who dressed in animal skins and who believed that in so doing they became that creature, seems hard to deny.

In view of this, it's perhaps less surprising to learn something about St Kentigern that the Christian church would rather forget: the fact that, according to his biographer Jocelyn, Kentigern owned a magic stick, probably shaped like a wand and made out of thorn. Experts have calculated that it would have been about three feet in length.

He was certainly not outdone by Merlin, who he allegedly confronted on several occasions. Their most famous encounter took place in the Caledonian forest in the Borders following the bloody battle of Arthuret in 573 AD, at which Merlin had been present but had then been forced into hiding after his side had been defeated. Merlin is described as a wild man of the woods, a pagan with the power of prophecy and ability to communicate with animals. But, as he lay dying, he asked St Kentigern to accept him into the Christian church. A piece of propaganda perhaps, but one which emphasises how important it was for the early Christians to overcome and absorb the old ways. Paganism didn't die, it simply became a part of Christianity.

The supernatural, so important in pre-Christian Scotland, in fact lives on in many surprising ways. Take Glasgow's coat of arms. It contains mystic symbols with magical origins of which few of us are aware. On the shield is depicted a bird, a tree, a fish and a hill. The bird sits on the tree, which grows from a hill. Resting against the tree is a fish. All four objects are linked to the mysterious individual we know as St Kentigern. The robin that the saint resurrected; the tree, a branch of which burst into flames at his command; the hill he raised by magic; and a fish whose inclusion in Glasgow's badge has its own strange origins.

The King of Strathclyde, Rhydderch Heal, asked for Kentigern's help to find a ring which he had given to his wife but which she had lost. The queen, Gwynedd, however, had in fact been having an affair and had given her lover the ring. Hearing rumours about his wife's dalliance, Rhydderch decided to test her faithfulness. Having, thanks to Kentigern, got hold of the ring he threw it into the River Clyde then he asked the queen to give him back the ring as proof that she had not been deceiving him. The queen, knowing that her life depended on retrieving it, also turned to Kentigern for help. Kentigern asked a monk to land the first fish that he saw. Having followed the saint's instructions, the monk found the queen's ring inside the salmon. It's another instance of Kentigern using his magical powers to influence events – saving a queen on this occasion. And once more we see a fish involved, that symbol which represents both the old and new religions. It was surely no accident that it played a role in this particular story and so is included in Glasgow's coat of arms.

Mysterious events lead to St Kentigern's last breath on earth. As he lay dying, he claimed that he was being visited by a spirit, who he described as an angel. The being encouraged St Kentigern to commit suicide. The angel not only promised to help with the saint's death but suggested that others might wish to die with him. On this entity's instructions a bath of warm water was prepared and, on 6 January 612, Kentigern, naked, stepped into it. His followers, crowded around the tub, watched as their leader seemed to drift into a strange sleep. He raised his hand one last time and then departed this life. His disciples took his body out of the bath and then fought with each other to get in before the water cooled so they could join Kentigern in the other world. A bizarre case of mass suicide.

By ending his own life Kentigern died in a way that would have resonated with the old pagan tradition but would strike today's Christians as downright odd. It demonstrates how different St Kentigern's view of the relationship between our world and that of the beyond was to our own. He was far closer to the pagan Merlin than one might suspect of a Christian saint, and in that way, Kentigern also had much in common with another saint, Columba.

St Columba

In her book *Ravens and Black Rain*, the author Elizabeth Sutherland described him as 'the father of second sight'. An apt title, but one that sits oddly on a man regarded as a founding father of Christianity in Scotland. Much of what is known about the life of St Columba derives from a biography written by St Adamnan, about a hundred years after Columba's death. And as with St Kentigern and Arthur, the supernatural played a key role in St Columba's life. Columba's preoccupation with the enchanted worlds may, however, reflect the background of his birth and the circumstances in which he was raised.

He was born on 7 December 521 beside Loch Garten in present day Ulster with royal blood in his veins, being descended from the kings of Donegal. He could also claim a blood link through his grandmother to the monarchs of the Argyll Kingdom who controlled much of the west coast of Scotland. In short, he was born into a world of privilege. But was he a druid as well? The priests of this pagan religion were still powerful in the Ireland of the sixth century. The country had not been conquered by invading Romans and so the growth of Christianity depended on the influence of individuals in persuading rulers to adopt the new religion. Claims made for the success of St Patrick's mission to Ireland in the fifth century must be taken with a pinch of salt, as the story was written up many years later by Christian writers who wished to wipe out any memory of druidic influence. It's more likely that during the period of Columba's upbringing, pagan ideas were still strong and influential. That certainly appears to be the case when we follow Columba's career.

It's noticeable that the name Columba, by which we call today the man originally known as Colum, means 'dove'. It's a bird well known for its connection to Christianity – the 'dove of peace' – and often used as a symbol in church literature. Less well known may be the fact that the dove was also sacred to the druids as a symbol of the soul. And once again, as with the fish, we have a creature whose significance, as a motif, passed from paganism to Christianity.

I'd suggest that it was no coincidence that he was given the name Colum, or Columba, nor that his first mission as a Christian missionary was to the ancient druidic oak grove at Calgaich on the northern Irish coast. Here he founded a monastery where Londonderry, or Derry, now stands. But, in spite of upholding the Christian religion, Columba revered the oak trees that grew there in the same way that the druids before him had regarded them as sacred, and he refused to cut them down. According to tradition, he deliberately chose the site of his monastery to avoid having to destroy the oak grove.

It represented a connection with the 'old ways' that he felt compelled to protect.

And when Columba headed for Scotland, it was another important druidic centre that he chose to make his base, the island of Iona. This spot had a long history as a mystic site and, given Columba's subsequent activities, it seems that he made it a deliberate choice. One particular part of the island may have attracted him. Situated in the centre of Iona, in an area of fertile land known as the machair, stands a fairy knowe or mound, the *sithean mor* in Gaelic. It sits prominently even today as a rising area of ground within a flat plain. It was a spot favoured by Columba, who regularly visited it. A site where he would stand for hours and communicate with entities he called 'angels'. According to his biographer, Adamnan, 'He saw, openly revealed, many of the secret things that have been hidden since the world began. Mysteries were revealed to him both of past ages and of ages still to come. Secrets unknown to other men'. In engaging in this practice, Columba was certainly copying the druid priests who saw it as part of their duty to enter into other worlds to see what the future might bring.

There are, in fact, at least fifty prophecies attributed to Columba. Adamnan states that one of his strange abilities was that of 'foretelling the future'. He described it as a gift from God, whereas with hindsight, we might suggest today that it was pagan practice under another guise. As a seer, Columba's predictions covered every kind of situation from the trivial to the significant. He warned a fellow monk that the book he was reading would fall into a tub of water. A short while later the monk got up in a hurry and dropped the book into a jug as Columba had foreseen. More serious were his prophecies of individual death and his reports of battles taking place at that very moment far away in Ireland and even in Italy.

But perhaps more than any other event connected to the saint it is his confrontation with the monster of Loch Ness that has stuck in popular memory. What are we to make of this story? Admirers of Columba were in no sense embarrassed by this strange encounter. On the contrary, they saw it as a great triumph and described it in considerable detail. At the time of the event, Columba was active in the lands of the Picts, no doubt engaged in the work of converting the pagans, the central focus of his life. When he reached the river Ness, which, of course, emerges from the Loch, he heard that a great water beast had been attacking anyone who attempted to cross the water. One man had recently been bitten and died. Columba asked one of his companions, Lugne Mocumin, to swim to the other bank and bring over a boat so that he could cross. Lugne did as Columba asked, but the monster rose up from the depths, and with its mouth wide open, made to attack him. Columba immediately made the sign of the cross in the air, calling on God's help, and at the same time shouting to the monster, 'Quick! Go Back!' Immediately the mysterious creature stopped its attack and vanished as quickly as it had arrived.

This incident has generated endless speculation. There's no way of proving that it really did happen, though it has the ring of truth about it. But if so, what was the creature they encountered? Nothing, according to scientists, fits the bill. However, it was certainly seen by Christians at the time as a great piece of propaganda, so you'd suspect that something, no matter how odd it seems to us, must have happened. Another explanation though, lies in the symbolic aspect. Paganism was often depicted by Christians as a monstrous animal, as in St Michael, or St George, slaying the dragon, the beast that represented the old religions. So, in this tale, Columba overcomes the 'old ways' in the shape of the monster of Loch Ness.

Evidence that the symbol aspect of the Loch Ness story was its main thrust comes from another, less well-known tale connected to the saint. While visiting the Island of Skye he was charged by a wild boar. Columba raised his hand and commanded the creature to die, and it fell dead on the spot. A miracle, certainly, but a boar was also a cult animal for the Celts and their pagan religion. It was, to them, a mystic beast. In killing the boar, Columba was also demonstrating the superior power of the Christian god over non-believers.

There are many weird stories linked to the life of Columba, but surely his decision to bury one of his followers alive outranks them all. A man named Oran was chosen for the venture. He was placed in a grave and left there alone for three days. When the tomb was opened Columba was apparently astonished to find that Oran was still alive. He appeared to be almost incoherent, but what he said was taken down and recorded. His words included the strange statement that 'there is no great wonder in death. Nor is Hell what it has been described'. One can be sure that Columba was not out to sacrifice one of his disciples. So that leaves only one other likely option, that he was sending Oran on a journey of some kind, the sort of mystic path to other worlds that pagans, even today in some societies, practise, a trip through space to the enchanted lands. It's hard to see what other aim Columba could possibly have had. Moreover, it fits with his own attempts to communicate with strange beings from the fairy mound on Iona, speaking with the 'angels' in the sky and the 'demons' or whatever phantoms that existed beneath the ground.

The impact on the Scottish psyche of Arthur, Kentigern and Columba was decisive. And there's no doubt, surprising though it may seem, that the three were linked by a chain of magic. Both Kentigern and Columba are connected to the Arthurian tradition and, to take one instance, are included in Mike Dixon-Kennedy's exhaustive compendium, *Arthurian & Celtic Myths & Legends*. They, in the company of Arthur, established the sense that the land of Scotland lay on the border of other realms, invisible to most but contactable by certain people, and in doing so influenced generations of Scots who followed.

It continued to be an important theme right up to the thirteenth century when the nation's greatest hero emerged, a man whose name resonates to the present, but could the supernatural really have played a key role in his life?

William Wallace

William Wallace died a cruel death. On 23 August 1305 at Smithfield in London he was first hanged by the neck till he lost consciousness. Cut down while still alive, his genitals were then hacked off and burnt in front of him. Wallace, it seems, was still breathing at this point and so, as Edward I had demanded, his chest and abdomen were cut open and his internal organs and heart removed. Wallace was then beheaded and parts of his body sent to various places around the country as a warning to those who the English king regarded as traitors. And in Edward's view, Wallace was a traitor, having led an uprising against him, the lawful, as Edward saw it, King of Scotland. Edward, nicknamed the 'Hammer of the Scots', never forgave Wallace for defeating his army at the Battle of Stirling Bridge on 11 September 1297. Edward had turned the tables on Wallace, however, and was blind to the possibility that the vicious death he inflicted on the man he had come to loathe would, in the long run, turn his hated adversary into an almost mythical figure. It is just as well he never lived to see it, for he would surely have detested such an outcome.

William Wallace is a Scottish hero of gigantic proportions. As the early twentieth-century Scottish Nationalist R.B. Cunninghame Graham wrote, 'Wallace made Scotland. He is Scotland. He is the symbol of all that is best in our national life.' No other figure in Scottish history can match the standing Wallace has achieved in popular affection. Not even Robert the Bruce. Is that because we love a failure? Because at the end of the day Wallace, unlike Bruce, did not lead Scotland to independence. He did win a great victory at Stirling Bridge. He did fight when others stood and watched. But in the final reckoning he died a captive of King Edward of England, and the forces he had attempted to lead to remove the hated invaders had simply withered away.

Was Wallace's mind truly on the job? Was there something in his character, in his view of the world that, though it inspired him in his struggle, made him less effective as a political and military leader? It's clear that there was another side to Wallace, a mystical side that historians either choose to ignore completely or at best play down as mere legend. But if the supernatural affected a way a great leader behaves, why bury it simply because it does not fit the way we would like that person to be remembered?

Wallace has been described as a shadowy figure, as given his immense reputation in Scotland and abroad – remember the impact of Hollywood's *Braveheart*? – it seems hard to believe that we know so little about him. He is viewed as a great fighter and leader of men, but maybe less adept at the art of politics.

Mysticism does not spring to mind when the activities of political or military leaders are considered, but it is more common than might be guessed. Elizabeth I of England had her white magician, John Dee, and Ronald Reagan took advice from an astrologer. Even great leaders, it seems, can embrace mysticism. It certainly envelops the figure of William Wallace. The supernatural was never far from his life and he even took advice from entities from other worlds.

The date of Wallace's birth and the place are shrouded in mystery. Various places have claimed the honour, and Elderslie near Glasgow is generally held to be the most likely. Even the date of his birth is unclear, although it is generally believed to be in 1270. The truth is that very little hard documentary evidence has survived about Wallace. We have only scanty information relating directly to his life. But what we do have is a strong oral tradition, much of which the poet known simply as Blind Harry incorporated into an epic narrative poem titled 'Wallace'. The poem, however, did not appear in print till 1477, long after William Wallace's death. Historians are divided about how reliable the poem is as history as it presents a view of Wallace as he was seen by ordinary Scots of the time.

From the opening lines a mystic image is presented of William Wallace, a stark contrast to the straightforward war leader we are familiar with. Wallace rose to prominence because of war. He played a key role in the 'Wars of Independence', an epic struggle to keep Scotland an independent nation against the attempt of Edward I of England to conquer the country. Problems began for Scotland when Alexander III, who had reigned since 1249, died in mysterious circumstances. It appeared that on a journey back from Edinburgh to Fife on a stormy night his horse slipped on the edge of a cliff path near Kinghorn. Alexander was found the following morning dead on the beach below with a broken neck. As bad luck would have it his successor, the Maid of Norway, died before she could succeed to the throne. There was now no obvious replacement, and thirteen people came forward to claim the crown, including John Balliol and Robert Bruce, the future King Robert's father.

For reasons unclear, Edward I was asked to choose between the competing claims and selected John Balliol. But Balliol and Edward fell out and the English king invaded and occupied Scotland. It was at this point that Wallace and others took up arms against the English to free the country.

Wallace was a fighter and ready to use sword and dagger to attack King Edward's men. But there was more to him than that. When Blind Harry described Wallace's first murderous encounter with the English, a fight with a man called Selbie, the son of the man in charge of Edward's forces occupying Dundee, two opposing facets of Wallace are presented immediately. Wallace stabs Selbie to death, as the man has insulted him. But, in the same line, Wallace is described as 'wearing a suit of green'. A suit of green! One only has to think of figures like Robin Hood, Herne the Hunter and other mythical figures to grasp that Wallace is here being presented as a man with a foot not only in this world but in the other world of mythical beings. And straight after this act Wallace heads for the shrine of St Margaret at Dunfermline Abbey and then to Dunipace near present day Denny, which at that time was regarded as one of Scotland's most mystical locations. Its name means 'hill of death' and it had been a sacred spot since pagan times. Why Wallace made for this place is a mystery, although it is said that he was in touch with a religious man of some kind. Could this have been some sort of shaman? It's certainly possible, as the area around the vast expanse that was Tor wood had a reputation as a haunt of the old religion with an ancient druidic past.

And even the Wars of Independence had opened in a supernatural atmosphere with a prophecy from the mystic

Thomas the Rhymer who lived between 1210 and 1290. In a vision, to which Patrick, Earl of March, was a witness, Thomas uttered these chilling words: 'Alas for tomorrow, a day of calamity and misery. Before the stroke of twelve a strong wind will be heard in Scotland, the like of which has not been known since times long ago. Its blast will dumbfound the nation. It will humble what is lofty and raze what is unbounding to the ground.' The following day, as Thomas had foreseen, the calamitous news of the death of Alexander III was reverberating round Scotland. The King had left no male heir to succeed him. War and disruption struck many, especially the powerful magnates, as a real possibility. And they weren't wrong.

When war between England and Scotland broke out and King John Balliol was deposed by Edward and Scotland was occupied by the English, it's worth noting that Wallace took up arms with the aim of making Balliol king again. He did not back Robert the Bruce because Bruce at this time was not vying to be king. Wallace steps into history as a freedom fighter with one famous act. In May 1297 he attacked and killed William de Heselrig, the local Sheriff and an Englishman, at his garrison in Lanark. It is said that this was in retaliation for Heselrig's murder of Wallace's wife Marion Brudefoote. Whatever the reason or the truth of the matter, Wallace was a marked man. He had killed one of King Edward's appointees and in his eyes was branded a traitor.

However, even if we accept the account that Wallace was goaded to act by the killing of his wife, it's clear that other factors may well have played a part in his decision to fight against England. One of the earliest accounts of Wallace's life describes how he visited Monkton Kirk in Ayrshire and went into a deep sleep or trance. In this shaman-like state Wallace had a vision. A man appeared who took hold of his hand. He gave Wallace a sword which 'glittered like glass', reminiscent of Arthur receiving Excalibur in some accounts. The figure also tells him that he 'must revenge [his] country's wrong', a clear indication that the other world was on Wallace's side.

Wallace was then taken to a mountain top and saw a brilliant ball of fire coming down from the sky. It moved towards him and then landed at his side. Out of the fire a woman appeared surrounded by a dazzling light. She handed Wallace a wand, coloured red and green, and, with a sapphire, made a sign across his face, usually interpreted as the saltire. Green is taken by some to indicate courage but it also has a very important other worlds significance, as its link to the nature spirits testifies. And blue? Certainly a colour associated with Scotland but also, in Scottish tradition, with the 'enchanted realms'. Red represents rebirth, as in the phoenix rising from the ashes, and also the bloody outcome of war and battle. This encounter can be interpreted on both the physical and spiritual level. In the final act of the encounter Wallace was given a book with gold, silver and brass lettering. At this the woman disappeared skywards in a blaze of light. The significance of the book has never been unravelled. Wallace started to read it but at that moment came to, suggesting that the book's contents were not the significant aspect of the gift.

Wallace meeting other world entities, and Wallace dressed in a mystical suit of green. Are these incidents simply coincidence? It might be reasonable to see it in this way if strange event did not pile on strange event. In one incident, Wallace was thrown over a castle wall in Ayrshire and assumed to have died. However, his childhood nurse heard what had happened and hurried from Ayr to find his body, which she did, and took it back to her house. At this point Thomas the Rhymer, the mystical prophet, arrived. Thomas announced that Wallace 'was not dead. If he be dead Thomas shall live no more'.

Thomas was not only referring to Wallace's physical death but his political and military death, as he went on to prophesy that Wallace, after many bloody battles, would drive the English out of Scotland and forever be remembered for it. Whether the Rhymer did meet Wallace may be debatable, but the key aspect is that visions and the involvement of mystical figures was seen as an important part of Wallace's life and campaign.

On another occasion, Wallace is described as praying to his guardian angels when he believes he sees a sign of approval, a glowing ball of flame hurtling through the sky. To Wallace, this was a sign from Heaven that it approved of what he was doing. It's a good example of how Christian practice and the supernatural could have overlapped in Wallace's beliefs.

And mysticism explains other incidents in Wallace's life which appear downright odd and irrelevant otherwise. According to tradition, Wallace was fishing at a spot where the Kilmarnock water enters the Irvine River and caught several fish. At this point, several soldiers working for Lord Percy came by and demanded all of his catch. Wallace refused, and in the ensuing melee, he killed the soldiers.

There's another odd incident involving Wallace and fish. He visited Ayr carrying a basket of fish when Lord Percy's steward demanded that he hand it over. Again, Wallace refused. A fight broke out and Wallace killed the steward. Of course, we may have here one incident that has over time developed into two. But the central theme is clear: Wallace is in charge of some fish, someone tries to take it from him, he refuses and the person who makes the demand is killed by Wallace. I would suggest that these events only make sense in a mystical context.

Fish have long been seen as mystic symbols, stretching back to the beliefs of ancient Egypt and beyond. The fish as a symbol was carried into Christianity and is still used to represent a belief in Jesus Christ. In this way the fish transcended both pagan and Christian religion and where it is used in the distant past it represents a mingling of the other world with this world. In supernatural terms, perhaps the most obvious embodiment is the Fisher King, the strange entity who in myth guarded the Holy Grail. He was, and is, a being who appears both pagan, as the ruler of the Otherworld, and Christian, because of the link to the Grail.

I would suggest that these incidents concerning Wallace and the fish can best be explained in this supernatural context. That Wallace is being linked to the Fisher King myth as the man who, quite literally, has protected *his* fish, the soul and the physical body of the people of Scotland.

How easily Wallace interacted with the realm of phantoms is described in an incident which occurred after one of the many minor battles that Wallace was involved in. Following the skirmish, Wallace took refuge at Gaskhall Castle. During the fight he slew a man called Faudon, who had behaved treacherously towards him, and cut off his head. But Faudon soon after reappeared, as if risen from the dead. A blast of a horn creating an unearthly noise aroused Wallace's apprehension. Its sound signalled something unusual and Wallace went to investigate. The undead stood in front of Wallace, holding its head, still spewing blood, in its outstretched hands. Wallace, terrified, drew his sword though he sensed it was pointless as he was facing some demonic figure. As it came towards him, Wallace turned and raced for a nearby river, no doubt well aware of the tradition that no phantom can cross running water. It was believed that the purity of nature would defeat the evil contained within any demon. Safely in the water, Wallace turned and saw the figure of Faudon standing on the ramparts of Gaskhall, surrounded by a ball of flame.

Wallace's greatest victory against Edward was at the Battle of Stirling Bridge on 11 September 1297. But the English war machine had not been defeated and the following year at the Battle of Falkirk, after a bloody encounter, Wallace and the Scots army suffered a decisive defeat. It was the end of organised resistance against Edward for the time being, and Wallace himself disappears into the shadows. We know that he remained active, trying to keep the struggle on the road, but his role as leader had melted away. When he re-emerged, it was as a captive.

The exact circumstances of his arrest in August 1305 are disputed. It appears that he spent the night of his capture in a barn on an estate belonging to Glasgow Cathedral, in the area now known as Robroyston. He was betrayed by a fellow Scot, Sir John Menteith, who arranged for soldiers to surround the barn and arrest Wallace. He was then transported secretly to England where Edward had him put on trial, determined to make an example of a man he regarded as a traitor. Wallace met his cruel end with courage.

Edward I has been seen as a man of war, but he was also superstitious. Is it going too far to suggest that the struggle against Edward can be seen in the context of the battle between the supernatural? Edward was determined to ensure that the powers of the other world be encouraged to assist his cause in Scotland. His seizure of the Stone of Scone, the mystical 'Jacob's Pillow', an object that entwined the Scots crown both with strange events recorded in the Bible and the myths of the ancient Egyptians, demonstrates his belief that the mystical aspect of the struggle was as important as its practical side. He also grabbed other supernatural artefacts, such as the Black Rood of Scotland. He was as susceptible to the belief in the power of magic as anyone. And against Wallace, albeit with the backing of a powerful war machine, his 'magic' triumphed.

The idea of Wallace the mystic has not survived into the

twenty-first century, but that does not mean that it should be forgotten. Wallace was a great freedom fighter, but there were other aspects to his character, an otherworldliness, which may have been as much an inspiration for his actions as his more practical desire to defeat King Edward I and to drive the English out of Scotland.

2

Demons and Deliverance

The supernatural had not always been viewed as a force for evil, but by the sixteenth century there had been a change in attitude. The Devil, it was believed, had a plan to take over Scotland using witches as his army of conquest. His influence, it was feared, was everywhere, with people resorting to black magic to murder and cause mayhem. Both Mary Queen of Scots and her son James VI were, in their different ways, to fall victim to the suspicion that Satan had taken control of people's minds. The result for Mary was tragedy, whereas James used it for his own benefit.

Robert the Bruce, on the other hand, represents a different aspect of the paranormal: the use of prophecy and prediction as a spur to action. Bruce lived a long time before witches were alleged to have the world in their grasp. But in the hands of a determined man that Robert certainly was, the paranormal could be as dangerous a weapon as any servant of the Devil.

Robert the Bruce

There may have been good reasons why Robert the Bruce wanted John Comyn dead. But why did he choose a church,

Robert the Bruce

© Getty Images

a most sacred site of the time, to carry out the murder? And why is there a persistent tradition that the mystical Knights Templar came to Bruce's aid at the Battle of Bannockburn? Compared to William Wallace, Bruce comes across as a more hard headed and cunning individual, one who had the ability to negotiate the political rapids that swirled through Scotland during the Wars of Independence. But, contrary to accepted opinion, he was also a man conscious of the effect that the supernatural would have on his success or failure to become King of the Scots.

Bruce came from a prominent, well-established family. He was born on 11 July 1274 into an aristocratic bloodline, one that had for generations owned extensive landed estates in south-west Scotland. As Lords of Annandale and Earls of Carrick, the Bruce family had built their stronghold at Lochmaben Castle situated on a neck of land running between two lochs. It may have been pure coincidence, of course, but Lochmaben has a long tradition as an ancient mystical centre. It may be one reason why the Bruce family selected it as their main base.

From the start of events leading to the wars between England and Scotland, the Bruce family were key players. Bruce's father, also called Robert, was sufficiently well connected to have a strong claim on the Scottish throne. He put his name forward, along with John Balliol, but was told on 6 November 1292 that his bid had been rejected. For as powerful a family as the Bruce clan this was not good news, and though they may have accepted Edward's decision to award Balliol the crown, it's noticeable that immediately following the failure of his bid that Robert the elder passed on his claim to the throne to his son, Robert the Bruce, and resigned his earldom also to his son. The wheels were rolling, but confrontation was still several years away.

Rivals to the Bruce family and big players in Scottish politics at this time were the Comyn family, who occupied many of the leading positions in government and had an extensive collection of estates and castles. A man who had their backing might well be in a good position to become king. If you found yourself their enemy, then your cause would probably be lost. So why did Bruce deliberately pick a fight with such a powerful clan, and enact a violent and shameful crime which he must have known would turn the Comyn crew against him, and which has stained his name for ever more? Robert the Bruce must have had not simply a good reason, but an overpowering one. I suggest that he did, and one that lies in the mystical realm.

It's always been a puzzle as to why Robert the Bruce, head of one of the most influential families in Scotland, chose to sign up with William Wallace in the fight against King Edward. Wallace was battling to make John Balliol, not Robert the Bruce, king. And when Wallace was defeated and resistance collapsed, he carried on the fight. Edward would not have dealt with Bruce as he dealt with Wallace. The Bruce family were too important and too noble to debase in the manner that Wallace had been. Edward I might have been the Hammer of the Scots, but politically he was no fool. He knew what he could get away with and what not to risk. In 1305 Bruce could most probably have made his peace with Edward, but he turned his back on it in the most dramatic way.

Was Robert the Bruce really seeking the backing of John Comyn in his bid to become king? Or did he have a more sinister motive right from the start? There were a number of witnesses to Bruce's outrageous act, one which shocked Christendom. But events began in an apparently innocent and friendly fashion. Robert the Bruce had arranged to meet with John Comyn. The site chosen was the Greyfriars Kirk in Dumfries, a convenient spot for both men. Exactly what was on the agenda is not clear, but it has been assumed that it related to Bruce's ambition to be king. The backing of the Comyn family would make Bruce's path to the throne that much easier. So on Wednesday, 10 February 1306, Bruce waited in the churchyard for John Comyn to arrive from Dalswinton Castle, some six miles away. And when he did, accompanied by his uncle Robert Comyn, Bruce behaved in a friendly manner, putting an arm round John and leading him into the kirk and up the aisle till they stood in front of the high altar.

What happened next is open to dispute, but there is no argument over the outcome. Bruce and Comyn appeared to get into an argument. It's not clear exactly over what, but it's suggested that as King Edward was old and likely to die soon, Bruce put it to Comyn that it might be a good moment to renew the fight against English occupation with the aim of making Robert king. Comyn refused. Bruce had suspicions that John had betrayed him to Edward and refused to listen to his denials. Suddenly Bruce attacked John Comyn, knocked him to the ground then struck him across the head with his sword. He walked out of the church, leaving the injured Comyn on the floor. Immediately one of his followers rushed over and finished Comyn off. John Comyn's uncle was also killed in the melee. There was now no going back for Bruce. It really was do or die.

But why did he do it? Even seven hundred years on it appears such a rash and unnecessary act. Bruce may have killed John Comyn, but there would be an army of Comyns desperate for revenge. Why deliberately provoke one of the most powerful families in Scotland? And Bruce rash? It was the only rash act he ever carried out and appears so contrary to his calculating nature that we must look to an extraordinary explanation to account for it. I believe that Bruce murdered Comyn to fulfil a prophecy.

Bruce and prophecy? They seem as different as chalk and cheese. However, during his campaign for the throne, Bruce found himself at one point in Argyll. There was an ancient prophecy, one so close to the hearts of the men of the Isles that Bruce decided it would bolster his propaganda war and rally support to him if he carried it out. He had his men haul his fleet of ships, with sails unfurled, roughly from modern West Tarbert to the better known ferry port of Tarbert. It was the shortest point between Loch Tarbert and Loch Fyne, but still represented a considerable feat involving several miles of tough work. Robert insisted that it be done, while he stood in one of the boats, to fulfil a prediction that whoever did this would 'win the Isles'. Of course, whoever won the control of the islands would also be King of Scotland. Robert undoubtedly took prophecy seriously.

In fact, at this time everyone took prophecy seriously and there were many accounts circulating about predictions made not only by current seers, but by long dead figures, Merlin and King Arthur being the most popular. One in particular gathered such force that it was written down and has survived to the present day. It foretold that following the death of Edward I, the 'covetous king', the people of Scotland and Wales, the Celtic tribes, would band together as independent nations and live in peace till the end of time.

Predictions were part and parcel of life. When Bruce was preparing in 1307 to sail with an invasion force from Arran to Carrick, a woman came up to him who claimed to be able to see into the future and told him that in a vision she had seen him crowned king. Given that much relies on oral tradition, it's difficult to be sure of what exactly happened, but it's undoubtedly true that the tradition of the supernatural was enmeshed with the Bruce family.

In 1148, a famous churchman of the time, St Malachy O'Moore, cursed Robert Bruce, an ancestor of the future king, for not sparing the life of a man sentenced to be hung. The curse was not only on Robert but on his offspring to the end of time. This act by the saint was widely reported and taken very seriously. It was even noted in England where years later it was reported that the curse had been so effective that three of Robert's heirs had died one after the other. It was in this atmosphere of belief in the power of the supernatural that Robert the Bruce operated. No surprise to learn, perhaps, that to end the curse and make peace with the saint, Robert the Bruce journeyed to the Abbey of Clairvaux where Malachy was buried, and donated three silver lamps which were placed in front of the saint's shrine. Money was handed over to ensure that the lamps would be lit and kept burning forever. And so, it was hoped, the spirit of Malachy would be placated and the curse be lifted.

When King Edward I took from Scotland the Black Rood of St Margaret, a jewelled relic case containing a piece of the cross of Christ, and the Stone of Scone, this wasn't simply an act of triumphalism. It was also an attempt to claim the supernatural influence associated with them for England. And deprive that power to the Scots. He had already, for the same magical reasons, grabbed the most sacred of Welsh relics, a fragment of the true cross called Y Groes Naid, or the Cross of Neath, and the crown of Arthur. As he battered his way across Scotland in 1296 he carried the Cross of Neath with him and forced leading figures to swear loyalty to him in its presence.

Prophecy and the supernatural was a powerful theme for those fighting for control of Scotland, and Bruce was ready to use it to the full. That's why he killed Comyn in such a brutal fashion. The best known seer at this time was Thomas the Rhymer, who lived from around 1210 to 1290, dates that overlap with the time that Robert the Bruce was alive. As previously mentioned, Thomas had famously predicted the death of Alexander III and the tragedy that was to unfold thereafter. He also reputedly predicted that Robert the Bruce would become king. That claim can certainly be disputed, as the predictions that he made were not written down till many years later, so it's unclear just exactly what was said by Thomas at the time. However, it's clear that Scotland was alive with prophecy and that the oral tradition was very strong. At a time when little was written down but people erected magnificent cathedrals and complex castles, what was said and memorised and passed on by word of mouth became a very important part of life. Thomas the Rhymer certainly lived. He was a well-known poet. He was a seer who was known to have made predictions about Scotland. One of these referred to a 'revenger king', a 'warlike heir' whose sword would 'sweat with blood' who would advance 'his kingdom's horn'. The word 'horn' in Scots referred to making oneself an outlaw, which Bruce certainly did when he murdered John Comyn, having been excommunicated by the Pope as well as having committed an obviously criminal act.

Of course, no one can be sure which prophecy may have influenced Bruce. There were many circulating, but they probably had a similar theme, that of a man who would carry out some significant act and by so doing propel himself into the front line of resistance against Edward I. Bruce certainly pushed himself to the fore at Greyfrairs Kirk. His deliberate murder of Comyn at the high altar has all the hallmarks of a ritual act, an event, as with the boat-hauling episode, which represented the fulfilling of some symbolic requirement. And this all could explain the persistent tradition that the Knights Templar, that shadowy and mysterious organisation, not only supported Robert the Bruce but were present at the Battle of Bannockburn.

In one sense, the Templars were neither shadowy nor mysterious. They were a long established organisation which had been set up in 1119 by Hugh de Payens and Godfrey of Saint Omer to defend pilgrims visiting the Holy Land and the city of Jerusalem. By the time of Robert the Bruce it had grown to a huge international affair owning an enormous number of properties, castles and religious buildings. But, again during Robert's lifetime, it all came crashing down. It was attacked by Philip IV of France on 14 September 1307, who ordered the seizure of all its property in France. The following month, on Friday, 13 October, leading Templars were arrested. It's not clear what led Philip to act as he did. The Templars were accused of various illegal and heretical practices, including worshipping the Devil. Just before they were arrested, it is claimed that many Knights Templar fled by ship to Scotland, taking with them considerable wealth and, equally important for Robert the Bruce, military expertise. In fact, there is a quite specific tradition held by the French Masonic Order that the records and wealth of the Templars were transported from La Rochelle to the Isle of May in the Firth of Forth. Investigations on the island have so far, however, revealed nothing of significance.

But this is where the Templars do become shadowy and Bruce's links with them mysterious. Why would a devout Christian link up with an organisation of alleged devil worshippers? Like the Knights Templar, Bruce too had been excommunicated, but he surely hoped that at some time this would be lifted. Would he risk alienating his Christian subjects by having a group involved in strange practices on his side?

But something was going on. If not directly by him then

on his behalf by his supporters. In December 1309, Bishop Lamberton, a strong ally of Bruce, invited Templar knights to a meeting in Holyrood Palace in Edinburgh. Given the struggle with England, coupled with the attack on the Templar organisation, it has been widely speculated that what was discussed was a pact or arrangement. If the Knights Templar supported Robert's campaign, the organisation would be allowed to continue its existence in Scotland. Although it might have seemed to be risking the wrath of the church, in fact Scotland had been excommunicated by the Pope, so technically the Templars here were exempt from his order. Still it's odd that Bruce would want to ally himself with an organisation that had the reputation of indulging in some strange beliefs and ritual practices.

Even odder that they appeared at the Battle of Bannockburn. But that is by tradition rather than proven fact. However, the Knights Templar had fought at the Battle of Falkirk in 1298, only sixteen years earlier, as two leading figures of the Order were killed on King Edward's side. So their presence at Bannockburn might make sense on the grounds that they were fighting for the freedom of a country, Scotland, where they believed they would be safe. Perhaps Bruce saw in their presence a mystical force that would help him carry the day. Is it coincidence that the Battle of Bannockburn was fought on 24 June, the anniversary of the birth of St John the Baptist, the saint most sacred to the Knights Templar, and a fact specifically referred to by Bruce in a speech to his men as they waited to attack? Would he have been prepared to risk a pitched battle against the mightiest war machine in Europe, the English army, if he did not have a belief that Saint John would be fighting on the Scots side? Of course, we will never know for sure, but Bruce may have truly believed that supernatural forces were with him on that fateful and famous day.

Mary Queen of Scots

But there is, unfortunately, always a dark side to the mystic realms. When eighteen-year-old Mary Stewart, on Tuesday, 19 August 1561, stepped from the ship that had brought her from France on to the dock at Leith shore to assume the role of Queen of Scots, she could scarcely have guessed what the future held. That within a few years she would be driven from her new kingdom, accused of using witchcraft to murder her husband Henry Stewart, the Lord Darnley. But was Mary really a follower of occult practices? There's no doubt that Scotland was awash with tales of witchcraft. Even the Protestant reformer John Knox was accused of using the black arts – how else could he have won the hand of the beautiful Margaret Stewart, a woman many years younger than he, if he had not used magic spells to entrance her? That claim, of course, could be put down to gossip and envy. More serious was the allegation circulating in the 1570s that in his youth he had been banished from St Andrews, where he had worked as a minister, for conjuring up the Devil. However, nothing came of this rumour either. Knox was too obviously a man of God for such dirt to stick. But across Scotland, people were being put to death for supposedly making a pact with Satan. The rise of witchcraft was taken so seriously that in 1563, in the second year of Mary's reign, an Act of the Scottish Parliament outlawed sorcery and necromancy and ordered the death penalty for anyone found guilty of forging a pact with the Devil.

This was not aimed against Mary personally, but she should perhaps have taken note of its passage into law and been a bit more careful about who she consorted with, for there's no doubt that at times the art of magic did come into the Queen's orbit. In June 1566, Mary experienced a difficult labour while awaiting the birth of her son, the future James VI. To relieve the Queen's agony the Countess of Atholl used her experience of witchcraft to transfer the pains Mary was going through on to Margaret, Lady Reres, who took to her bed and appears to have suffered exactly as her mistress was doing. It's not clear, however, whether Mary benefitted from this act of sorcery, though James was certainly born a healthy child and the Queen made a quick recovery from her difficult childbirth. Countess Atholl, lady-in-waiting to Mary, was openly spoken of as a woman who was well versed in magic lore, having studied with an expert. But whether or not she had made a pact with Satan, no one could say. To be fair to Mary, the use of charms and magic tokens in childbirth, a dangerous and uncertain event for both woman and child, was practised throughout the land. However, those surrounding Mary and others she was connected with may have had a more sinister agenda. So why did Mary become involved with them?

Most notorious was her relationship with James Hepburn, the fourth Earl of Bothwell. The family held extensive lands in East Lothian and their main residence was Crichton Castle, near the modern town of Pathhead. Bothwell had been born in 1535, several years before Mary, and had drive and ambition. Some said he aimed to be King of Scotland. He was also alleged to be an expert practitioner of the black arts. Bothwell had spent some years in France on the face of it to improve his education. It was claimed, however, that he had spent his time there learning about sorcery and magic and that he was now using his expertise to ingratiate himself with the Queen.

Bothwell didn't help matters by his association with Janet Beaton. She had a reputation for occult practices that outranked even his. When he was twenty-four, he took her as his mistress, though she was many years older than he was and some judged that it was a union of the black magicians. She was a beauty whose looks never faded, was never short of lovers and who survived five marriages – the last when she was sixty-one. It was well known that she had achieved all this through the use of magic spells. She also, however, had a link to Queen Mary. Janet Beaton was the sister of Lady Reres, the same woman who had taken upon herself the childbirth pains of the Queen. Lady Reres was also the aunt of another of Mary's ladies-in-waiting, the well-known Mary Beaton, one of the four Marys celebrated in poem and song. This would turn out to be a lethal entanglement of relationships.

But perhaps Mary would have remained free of allegations of using witchcraft if she had not taken it upon herself to marry Henry, Lord Darnley. There were good reasons for doing so. Mary, brought up in France and having been married to Francis II of France, was a staunch Roman Catholic. She now found herself back home in Scotland, monarch of a country which was staunchly Protestant. Marrying Darnley, also a Catholic and an Englishman with a very strong claim on the throne of England, probably seemed at first glance a sensible move. It would provide her with support as the ruler of Scotland. There would be a man to share the burden, and at the time it was very much a man's world. It would also strengthen her claim, which she had in her own right, to become Queen of England. Unfortunately, it turned out a disastrous decision.

Henry Darnley was tall and good-looking, but there was little beyond that to commend him. He was immature, rash and little interested in the details of government. He wanted to be King, but not to suffer the responsibilities of ruling a country. Mary married Darnley on Sunday, 29 July 1565 at a ceremony held in the Chapel Royal at Holyrood. She was twenty-three; he was just nineteen. She was soon to regret her decision. Mary quickly realised that her new husband and king was not up to the job. She cut him out of decision-making and, in effect, sidelined him. Darnley did not understand why Mary was treating him, as he saw it, in an off-hand manner and why she was excluding him from government. He became resentful and suspicious and was easy prey for older, more devious individuals with an agenda of their own. Several leading lords of the land were keen to get rid of Mary. And anyway, they said, wasn't she in league with that notorious witch, the Earl of Bothwell? Even sharing his bed?

Events came to a head on Saturday, 9 March 1566 with the murder of Mary's Italian secretary David Rizzio at the Queen's apartment in Holyrood Palace. Darnley was undoubtedly involved in this plot, though the lead was taken by Patrick Lord Ruthven, a notorious warlock, which shows that witchcraft was never far away from the affairs of the Scottish Court. The unfortunate Rizzio was killed as Mary was enjoying a late supper, even as she looked on stunned and horrified. Pregnant with her son, Mary had a knife held against her body and must have feared for her own life. She could never, however, be accused of cowardice and her nerve held throughout the shocking ordeal. Although Darnley tried to distance himself from the murder – and Rizzio had suffered over fifty stab wounds – from that moment on Mary utterly despised her husband and suspected him of wishing her own death and that of their child so that he could become king in his own right. If he had involved himself in the plot only out of jealousy of her supposed close relationship with Rizzio then Mary despised him for his failings as a man as well. There can be little doubt that following this event Mary wanted to end her marriage to Darnley. But did she resort to witchcraft and murder to achieve it? Rumours certainly flew around over her alleged knowledge of the black arts. She had spent years at the French Court, notorious for its lax moral standards and involvement in sorcery. Her former husband Francis II's mother, Catherine de Medici, was well known to consult astrologers, and even worse. Mary could not escape being tainted by her background.

But the circumstances of Darnley's death undoubtedly raise suspicions. On Christmas Eve 1566 Darnley attended the baptism of James at Stirling Castle, apparently in good health. He left immediately after, heading for Glasgow with those he trusted, as he believed that there were people around Mary who would be glad to see him dead. He was less than a mile out of Stirling when, according to information recorded at the time, 'a violent disorder suddenly struck every part of his body'. And by the time he reached Glasgow he was covered in 'livid pustules'. He was in so much pain that he was not expected to survive. But he did live, though he suffered even more bizarre and unpleasant symptoms. His body was covered in black pimples. He sweated continuously and stank unbearably. His hair fell out. And the symptoms continued for several weeks. Even today it is unclear exactly what Darnley was suffering from. Both smallpox and syphilis have been suggested, though there is nothing conclusive. It was certainly a convenient event for his enemies. It was known that Darnley was planning to leave the country and the suspicion on Mary's part was that he was up to no good. His sudden illness scuppered that project and forced him to remain in Scotland, to the benefit of those who were out to finish him. So fortuitous was the illness that now, as then, it has been suggested that Darnley was poisoned while at Stirling Castle. Poison suggests black magic, as rituals would have been used to make the potion more effective. And later events suggest that this is what is likely to have happened.

Darnley however, against expectation, gradually recovered. It's a mystery though why he agreed to return to Edinburgh, as urged to by Mary. He certainly hoped to resume marital relations with her, even pleading that he had learnt from his mistakes. Mary was not convinced of his sincerity and suspected him of planning to murder her. She maybe had a good reason for wanting Darnley back in the capital where she could keep an eye on him, but it was also a convenient spot in which to carry out his murder.

Accompanied by Mary, Darnley, carried on a litter, arrived in Edinburgh around the 30 January 1567. He had only a few days left to live. It was originally intended that the King would stay at Craigmillar Castle, then on the outskirts of the city, to complete his recovery, but Darnley objected and was accommodated at the Old Provost's House at Kirk o' Field, a country house on the edge of the city but just within the Flodden Wall which surrounded the capital. In the light of later events exactly who chose Kirk o' Field as a residence for Darnley has been the subject of much debate which has never been resolved. I would suggest, however, that the plot to blow up the Old Provost's House was only part of the plan, the icing on the cake of a process that was already well under way: to kill Darnley by witchcraft.

It has been remarked that Mary was very concerned over Darnley's health. She even offered to bathe his body herself to aid his recovery and had ordered that some of her own linen be cut into strips to put inside the King's nightshirt, probably around the collar and so next to the neck. That act alone should cause those versed in the ways of witchcraft to pause for thought. Placing next to someone's body an item imbued with some evil force was a classic method of the time to bring about death by black magic. Accused witches were executed for carrying out just such acts. Mary's son, James VI, would have his life threatened in the very same manner by followers of Satan. And there are other odd incidents which have puzzled historians, but in the context of witchlore make sense.

In a letter to the Earl of Bothwell, her alleged lover and future husband, Mary wrote:

This day I have wrought till two of the clock on this bracelet, to put the key in the cleft of it, which is tied with two laces. I have had so little time that it is very ill, but I will make a fairer; and in the meantime take heed that none of those that be here do see it, for I have made it in haste in their presence. I have not seen him [Darnley] this night for ending your bracelet, but I can find no clasps for it. It is ready thereunto, and yet I fear lest it should bring you ill hap, or that should be known if you were hurt. Send me word whether you will have it.

Why, it has been wondered, was Mary making such a big thing of this bracelet and so worried that if anyone knew about it, it would cause problems for Bothwell? Why did she specifically warn him not to let anyone see the bracelet? Mary was always handing out gifts, as monarchs are obliged to do, so why was this one any different? It only makes sense if it was linked to something sinister, if it was, in fact, meant to be used in some occult way. An item that could be used to get close to Darnley, an object that he might, for example, wear. It would require that it contained an item that had come in contact with the intended victim, and Mary quite specifically mentions the 'two laces' attached to it. Why on earth mention such details to Bothwell? Only, of course, if it was to let him know that the spell had been completed. If it had been meant simply as a gift to him there would have been little reason to describe the item to him. The present would speak for itself.

And linked to this is an enigmatic exchange between Mary and Darnley which took place in Glasgow while he was recovering from his illness. Mary had been visiting him on his sickbed and chatting with him. She suddenly asked him if he liked Lady Reres, the woman who had infamously taken on her birth pains, and if he was annoyed with her. Darnley replied that he knew little about her and was clearly puzzled by the question. Why did Mary mention Lady Reres? She was, of course, the sister of Janet Beaton, the well-known sorceress and mistress of another alleged black magician, the Earl of Bothwell, with whom, there can be little doubt that, Mary had by now formed a strong bond. At this distance in time, we can only speculate what Lady Reres' part in the plot was to be, but it may be that Mary intended that she might use her in some way if Darnley was not suspicious of her. And he clearly harboured no misgivings at all about Lady Reres. But perhaps the details of the plan changed. Or maybe she played a part which has so far remained undiscovered.

One fact is clear though. At around 2am on Monday, 10 February 1567, a massive explosion blew the Old Provost's House at Kirk o' Field apart. Most of the building was reduced to rubble. Darnley, however, who was known to have retired to bed around midnight, was nowhere to be found though the mutilated bodies of two of his servants were quickly discovered lying in the wreckage. The Queen's husband was not located for another three hours. Around 5am he was discovered lying almost naked on his back beneath a pear tree in a garden about sixty feet from his former bedroom. His hand was lying across his genitals, a bizarre gesture of modesty, which, naturally, aroused suspicion because, despite the severity of the detonation, there was not a mark on Darnley's body. There were no obvious burn marks. No bruising, which might have occurred had the body been thrown a distance. No evidence of a physical assault such as strangulation.

Beside Darnley lay the body of his valet William Taylor. It was also unmarked and he looked as if he'd simply laid down for a rest beside his master. The state of both men did not match the event. There's no doubt that both had gone to bed in a house that had been through a massive explosion. But their appearance suggested they had not died in the cataclysm. They had clearly been murdered in some other way. But again the absence of any physical damage added to the mystery.

How the destruction of the Old Provost's House was carried out has been the subject of much speculation. The problem of taking into the building the vast quantity of gunpowder that would have been needed to produce such a huge effect without Darnley or his servants spotting it has never been satisfactorily explained. It's a complete mystery. And if witchcraft was used to achieve it, as was rumoured at the time, then no one came forward to boast of their magical powers. That the explosion was carried out to conceal the murder seems certain. To use gunpowder to kill Darnley was surely a risk too far if the plotters wanted to make sure he died. It seems highly likely that black magic was being used against Darnley, either to kill him outright or to weaken him physically and mentally for the coup de grâce. The explosion was meant as a fig leaf, but the bodies left quite deliberately in the open to implicate others. There was clearly a plot within a plot.

And Mary was the next intended victim. Although she appeared distressed by Darnley's death, that did not prevent rumours circulating implicating her in the events. By 16 February, only a week after the explosion, placards appeared on buildings across the city. The notices claimed that Mary had agreed to the murder of her husband, which had been carried out by Bothwell, and stated that the witchcraft of Janet Beaton, the Lady of Buccleuch, had been used in the assassination. And things got worse for Mary. On 1 March more placards appeared, this time showing Mary as a mermaid, naked from the waist up wearing a crown, alongside

Bothwell, depicted as a hare crouching in a circle of swords. The use of a mermaid to describe Mary was deliberately intended as an insult, as it suggested a siren who lured men to their doom and was commonly in use at the time as a term for a prostitute. The hare was the crest of the Earls of Bothwell. To the Scottish public, the meaning was clear: Mary was protecting her lover and murderer of her husband. That, of course, is not the whole story as this famous placard can be seen to have a deeper meaning. The supernatural was wrapped up in Darnley's death, either in reality or simply as belief. The mermaid, used to represent Mary, was an image of the other world, a phantom figure with strange, mystic powers. And the hare, Bothwell's badge, had long been linked to the occult. It was favoured by witches when they wished to turn themselves into an animal of some kind. Those on trial for sorcery had often been accused of doing just exactly that. The connection with the black arts implied in these drawings would not have been lost on our ancestors.

The murder of Darnley had set in motion a train of events that finished Mary's reign. She married Bothwell, her third husband, but this was too much for the people of Scotland, who joined those leading figures of the land who wanted to see Mary gone. Although not without her supporters, there were too many against her and in 1568 she was forced to flee to England where she suffered eventual execution at the hands of her cousin Elizabeth I.

If Mary was involved in witchcraft then she didn't manage to save herself. Nor did the Earl of Bothwell, who ended as an exile abroad. Of course, there were those who would argue that they were beaten by those better versed in the power of the occult. But there's a curious fact that rarely seems to be mentioned. Why was Darnley's body placed deliberately beneath a pear tree? When Mary had visited Darnley in his sickbed, she commented to him that it was around twelve months since the death of David Rizzio. This had puzzled Darnley. Why had Mary mentioned it now? Was she trying to tell him something? In Scottish folklore the pear tree had a particular significance. It was said to relive past dramas. Perhaps it was intended as a sign that the death of Rizzio had, for Mary, finally been avenged.

King James VI

The Queen passed into history as a tragic figure, but the black arts lived on to place a terrible burden on her son and successor. King James VI was in a dark and fearful mood. 'I pray God', he wrote, 'to purge the country of these devilish practices for they were never so rife in these parts as they are now.' These words appeared in *Demonology*, the book the King wrote in 1597 to justify his belief in the power of witchcraft and as a guide to discovering and exterminating those involved in the black arts, but what strange events had brought him to this stage of despair? Could the ruler of a country truly believe in the power of witches and that one of his own relatives was a practitioner of the occult?

The lives of King James VI and the fifth Earl of Bothwell, Francis Stewart, were closely entwined. They were related as cousins, and a part of the ruling elite who governed Scotland and set the trend by their behaviour. They were also both firm believers in the power of the supernatural. That's not surprising, as many key members of upper-class Scottish society consulted magicians and sorcerers to cure illnesses and to predict their future. Some, however, used it for more sinister purposes, a fact that King James was well aware of. His mother, Mary Queen of Scots, after all, had been accused of using witchcraft to murder her husband Henry Stewart, Lord Darnley. But she was following a well-established tradition.

In 1479 the Earl of Mar was accused of trying to kill his brother King James III by witchcraft and in 1537 Lady Glamis was burned alive for using magic charms against King James V. Throughout James' formative years the use of the black arts to remove leading figures was an ever-present theme. In 1568, when James was only twenty-two, Sir William Stewart, Lyon King of Arms, was executed for worshipping a spirit called Oberon and for using sorcery in an attempt to murder the Earl of Moray, Scotland's Regent and leading political figure of the day. In 1577 Violet Mar, a Perthshire witch, was charged with using 'sorcery, witchcraft and invoking spirits'. She admitted that her intention had been to kill the Earl of Morton, who had taken over as the country's Regent. It's unclear whether anyone else was involved in Violet's plot, though Morton may have suspected that she was not acting alone. And when even the Archbishop of St Andrews, Patrick Adamson, was summoned in August 1583 to appear before his local kirk, accused of consulting witches when he had fallen ill, it reveals the extent to which the belief in the power of magic and those who practised it ran through the whole of society from top to bottom. The Archbishop escaped punishment, as did many high-ranking figures who broke the terms of the 1563 Witchcraft Act by consulting astrologers, sorcerers and witches, but witchcraft coupled with treason was an entirely different matter.

So Francis Stewart, the fifth Earl of Bothwell, should perhaps have exercised more care over who he consorted with and what he consulted them on. His family had a reputation to live down. It was Francis's uncle, James Hepburn, the fourth Earl of Bothwell, who had formed a deadly alliance with Queen Mary and who had earned a reputation as a notorious witch.

He had been driven out of Scotland and, in 1578, ended his life in captivity in a Danish prison. Francis, it might have been thought, viewing his uncle's career, would have been anxious to avoid any taint of black magic, or political ambition, but he seems to have inherited his uncle's unstable and rebellious nature.

Only three years older than the King, having been born in 1563, Francis had a strong claim to be part of James' governing circle, maybe even on the crown itself. His father, John Stewart, had been an illegitimate son of King James V, so the blood of royalty flowed in his veins. As a kinsman of James VI, Bothwell might have expected that by right he would be consulted by the King. However, for whatever reason, ambition no doubt providing the key motive, in 1589 Bothwell led an uprising against the King, a rebellion which rapidly collapsed. He was not a man people automatically trusted, a sense of waywardness seemed to ooze from his personality.

But James did not deal harshly with his untrustworthy cousin. Instead, in the autumn of 1589 Bothwell was appointed as a member of the Council of Regency, set up to govern Scotland while the King travelled to Scandinavia to bring back his new bride, Anne of Denmark. A more stable man might have built on this promotion, but instead Bothwell began to fret over a prophecy that he had received from a sorcerer in Italy that said the King planned to execute him. He took this prediction seriously and began consulting a well-known witch and magician, Richard Graham, to discover James' real attitude towards him and ways in which he could keep the King's favour. It could also, of course, have provided Bothwell with a motive to kill the King and take the crown for himself.

Meanwhile, strange events surrounded the planned marriage of King James to Anne. The new queen had sailed out of Copenhagen on 5 September 1589, heading for Scotland, but had been driven onto the coast of Norway by strong winds. An impatient James decided to travel to Denmark and collect his new bride, but storms stopped him from leaving till 22 October. Though he reached Scandinavia and brought Anne back, mists and more storms delayed his arrival at Leith until 1 May. Even as the new couple made the journey across the North Sea accusations were being made in the Danish capital that acts of witchcraft had stirred up bad weather, perhaps with the intention of drowning the King and Queen. Several women were arrested on the instruction of Copenhagen's governor, put on trial and executed for using sorcery in an attempt to block Anne's journey to Scotland. James may have been disturbed by the news, but at this point did not appear to suspect that witchcraft had been involved and saw the stormy weather as no more than a natural peril of the sea. He was soon to change his mind.

In Scotland, events were being set in motion that would soon cause a political maelstrom. Agnes Sampson, a middle-aged woman from Nether Marshall, a village near Haddington in East Lothian, was well known as a witch and was often consulted for cures when illness struck. However, in April 1589 an attempt was made by the local kirk to have Agnes arrested for witchcraft. For the moment nothing came of it, but Agnes was soon to play a key role in allegations of treason and black magic which would rock leading figures in the government of Scotland, including the King himself. No one though could have expected the political earthquake that would follow had they been in Tranent that November 1590. Accusations of witchcraft were rife and when David Seton, a depute baillie of the village, began to suspect his servant, Gillie Duncan, of using black magic, it was by no means a unique event. He was seeking to explain why Gillie had suddenly earned a reputation for curing the sick, and why she kept disappearing at night. On his own authority he arrested her and carried out a physical examination. On her body he discovered what he believed to be the mark of the Devil. Torture with thumbscrews and a knotted rope then brought a confession from Gillie that she had indeed been involved in witchcraft. She named several others who had been part of the coven. Agnes Sampson was one. John Fian was another.

John Fian was, on the face of it, a simple country schoolteacher who lived close to Tranent, in the village of Saltpans. However, it seems that Fian also acted as secretary to the Earl of Bothwell and so a link was quickly established to a more rarefied area of society. But, on its own, it proved nothing, and the ripples that were spreading out might have also come to nothing had Bothwell not been under suspicion and shown himself to be a more stable character. By this time James was having doubts over his cousin's intentions and there were certainly those in governing circles who saw the Earl as an outright threat. But was there a plan to involve Bothwell in a witchcraft plot? Was he really the head of a coven of witches? Or did the unfortunate Earl stumble into trouble through his own carelessness? Centuries later, the debate rumbles on.

Agnes Sampson, through her confession, convinced James that there was a plot to kill him. There had, she explained, been several attempts. The storms that had delayed the King's departure to Denmark and had greeted his fleet on his return had been caused by the coven's witchcraft. A cat had been tied up and then taken out to sea and thrown into the water while James' name and incantations were uttered. As that had failed, a fresh act of magic was set in motion. A picture of James had been stolen then wrapped in a roll of cloth. At a gathering of witches at Acheson's Haven, along the coast from Prestonpans, the bundle was passed round a circle of witches who kept repeating 'James the Sixth'. Agnes then handed the picture to the Devil, who she described as being dressed in dark clothes and wearing a cloak, and asked him to bring about the death of King James. The destruction of the picture would achieve this end, if the magic had been carried through properly and Satan played his part. At this gathering, the Devil's presence inescapably branded those attending as agents of Satan, which was unfortunate for Bothwell, as his name was also linked to the event as apparently Agnes stated that he had promised to provide them all with gold, silver and refreshments.

James, hearing this tale in person from Agnes, as she had been brought to Holyrood Palace on 5 December 1590 to repeat her story, might still have doubted it had a bizarre event not occurred. Agnes asked him to lean forward and then whispered in his ear the words that James had spoken to Queen Anne on their first night together. James was stunned. He couldn't explain how Agnes could have known what he said, as he had told it to no one else. 'By the living gods', he gasped, 'all the devils in Hell could not have discovered the same.' In a moment he was convinced that Agnes must be telling the truth; in the same moment, Agnes had sealed her own fate and that of the others connected to her, and one of those was the Earl of Bothwell, who had been known to consult Agnes, not only to cure illness which would have been overlooked, but on more risky matters including the state of the King's health and the length of his reign. Why, it was asked, was he so keen to learn these facts?

Bothwell, who was well informed of events, was growing nervous, sensing that James had him in his sights. He retired to his castle at Crichton to await developments. They didn't bring good news. No doubt, he could have glossed over it all if his name had not kept cropping up linking him to those connected with the witch covens. John Fian, who had been mentioned by Gillie Duncan as one of Satan's followers, a fact corroborated by Agnes Sampson, was a known associate of Bothwell's. What he admitted to pushed the Earl to the centre of the stage. According to a pamphlet of the time, 'News from Scotland', Fian was severely tortured to force a confession from him. His legs were strapped into a device called the Spanish Boot – metal casings clamped around each leg which were then battered with a hammer to cause terrible pain. Fian, however, held out until an examination revealed that two pins had been pushed into the roof of his mouth, a witch's spell that allowed him to endure the pain that he would otherwise have suffered. Once the pins were removed, Fian's resolve collapsed and, with James as a witness, he wrote down a confession describing his involvement with the witch coven.

It turned out that Fian was a key member of the coven which met at North Berwick Kirk and had been appointed by Satan to be his secretary. His duties were to record the coven membership, issue oaths of obedience and pass on the Devil's orders to his followers. He sat beside Satan and walked with him in their ritual ceremony around the churchyard, going anti-clockwise to cleanse the cemetery of its Christian sanctity. A major gathering of witches had taken place there on 31 October 1589, All Hallows Eve. Fian described how Satan had led the coven into the graveyard and, standing over a grave, bent a hand towards the ground, which opened to reveal a fresh corpse. At a signal from the Devil the coven pulled the body from its grave and hacked off the arms and legs. The limbs were later used in a ceremony at Leith in an attempt to sink the King's ship. For his involvement with Satan, Fian was burned as a witch on 13 January 1591.

But Fian's death came too late for Bothwell. The

schoolmaster had acted as both Satan and the Earl's secretary. The connection was obvious and, it was rumoured, Bothwell might even be the Devil himself in human form. Or acting the role of Satan to deceive the coven. Either way, it branded him as a witch and one with links to a coven whose members had set out to kill the King.

But it was his association with Scotland's most famous sorcerer, Richard Graham, which sealed his fate. Graham made no secret of his magical practices and was consulted by many well-known people. Unfortunately for both him and Bothwell, he was linked to the North Berwick witches and so to treason, as it was said that he was the one who had arranged for the coven to assemble, using Gillie Duncan as a messenger. And Bothwell could not deny knowing Graham, though he attempted to play down the extent of their association. What is interesting is that Richard Graham, a man who blatantly flouted the Witchcraft Act, was so well connected. Bothwell claimed to have met him in the Chancellor of Scotland's house, where Graham showed both of them an 'enchanted stick'. There was a widely circulated account of how the sorcerer had raised the Devil in the backyard of Sir Lewis Bellenden, a Lord of Session, and a leading figure of the time.

Richard Graham certainly moved in rarefied circles, but on this occasion his connections would not save him. It may be that he was seen as a useful tool to bring Bothwell down. Accusations against the Earl of Bothwell were now brought into the open and he was accused of conspiring with Richard Graham to murder the King by magic. In November 1590 Graham was locked up in the Edinburgh Tolbooth. He later claimed that during his time there Bothwell sent him money to ensure his silence. It may be true, but there's no doubt that pressure was being brought to bear on Graham and that he was being warned that if he refused to incriminate Bothwell he would lose his own life.

According to Graham, Bothwell consulted him regularly following the prediction from the Italian sorcerer that he was out of favour with James and that his life was in danger. He asked Graham how he could save himself. The magician explained that he had consulted a coven of witches who decided that the best way was to concoct a witch potion that, placed over a spot James would pass through, would drip on his head and kill him by the power of its spell. Alternatively, a wax figure of the King could be made, combined with various magic ingredients, which when placed in a fire would destroy the King as it melted in the heat. If Bothwell had considered these options he could not escape being found guilty of a charge of treason. One fact that told against him were his denials that he had been closely associated with Graham. The evidence suggested that they had met regularly, a fact confirmed by Ninian Chirnside, an employee of Bothwell's, who had arranged the meetings. He alleged that there had been at least twenty meetings that he knew of. The general opinion of the time was that Bothwell was such an unstable and strange character that it was more than likely that he had been involved in such a bizarre plot.

Bothwell was eventually brought to trial on 15 August 1593, although the charges against him dated from two years earlier. He had managed to escape and spent some time in Caithness, far from the King's clutches. It's probable that he only agreed to stand trial when he was sure that he would be acquitted. Richard Graham had already been executed in March 1592 in spite of assurances he had received to the contrary, so this key witness for the prosecution could not appear in person. Nor could John Fian, Agnes Sampson, and Gillies Duncan, all of whom would have been likely to testify against him but had shared Graham's fate. There were still their confessions, of course, but Bothwell could, and did, denounce them, claiming that in Graham's case the magician had been induced to accuse him by leading figures in the King's circle who were out to destroy him.

At the end of a nine-hour trial which lasted from 1pm to 10pm, Bothwell, tried by a jury of his peers, was found not guilty. He had made sure of the verdict, packing the court and the capital with his friends, relatives and supporters. Had it gone the other way, there would undoubtedly have been a serious disturbance and James' own safety might have been threatened. But Bothwell was finished as a political force. James would never trust him, and his actions were widely seen as rash and foolish. Like his uncle, James Hepburn, the fourth Earl, Bothwell was forced to leave Scotland and lived out his days in Italy.

And out of these weird events came James' *Demonology*, which famously, or not-so-famously, defended the belief in the reality of witchcraft to the extent that, he argued that, 'no sex, age nor rank' should 'be exempted' from being put to death if found guilty of forming a pact with the Devil. That may have been intended as a justification for the executions that took place during his own reign, but he certainly, for a time at least, believed that the agents of Satan posed a threat to the nations of Christendom. And he could speak from personal experience – even his own cousin had been a witch.

3

Science, War, Writers and Black Magic

No aspect of human activity escapes the influence of the supernatural. Its use in literature appears the most obvious, as shown in the lives and works of Robert Burns, James Hogg and Sir Walter Scott, but it can also be a useful tool in war, as the career of Bonnie Prince Charlie demonstrates. Nor can science escape its impact. In fact, as the life and death of Hugh Miller proves, it can cause a challenge to the mind that can prove fatal.

Robert Burns

The day had arrived to move the body of Scotland's most famous poet, Robert Burns, from the pauper's grave which held him in a Dumfries churchyard to the mausoleum that had been specially built to hold the remains of the now world-renowned figure. However, when the coffin was opened a shock awaited those gathered round. Instead of the rotted corpse that they had expected to find, Burns' body lay as fresh as the day in which it had been interred, his face a picture of serene calm, as if all the worries that had come his way during his lifetime had disappeared in death. Some took it as a sign, a supernatural event that had preserved the flesh of a man who had himself been obsessed with the world beyond the grave, as, among other events, his creation of the epic poem 'Tam o' Shanter', with its theme of encountering ghosts and witches demonstrates. As they leant over to lift his body, however, it disintegrated in an instant, leaving only a collection of bones and a scattering of dust. It could, of course, be taken as a sign that paranormal incidents are part and parcel of life but when we reach out to touch them they disappear before our eyes, leaving us more puzzled than before.

During his life Burns tried to explore the supernatural. He had grown up with it. He certainly believed that a strange event had heralded his arrival in the world. A comet appeared, and could be seen, around the time of his birth on 25 January 1759. In those days such an event coinciding with the arrival of a baby was seen as an omen. People could argue whether it was good or bad, but it was accepted that it was a matter of undoubted significance, either way. In later years, Burns himself admitted, 'I am naturally of a superstitious cast'. Does this explain why he was attracted to the Freemasons, a society he was a member of till his death in 1796? He certainly grew up in an atmosphere immersed with supernatural lore.

Born in the village of Alloway in Ayrshire, about two miles from the town of Ayr, to a struggling tenant farmer, the rational mind which dismissed ghosts and phantoms had to contend with local beliefs that the spectres of the other world were all around – and visited us. Alloway Kirk, not far from Burns' two-roomed birthplace, in particular, was a known haunt of strange creatures of the night.

Burns was introduced to the supernatural at an early age. Betsy Davidson, who he described as 'an old maid of my mother's' had a vast store of supernatural tales, incidents which had occurred in the area he grew up. These stories disturbed him to such an extent that throughout his life he could never escape the sensation that spirits of the dead and phantoms from other worlds were hovering around him. It was these early tales, he admitted, that fired his poetic imagination. But as a thinking man, they also intrigued him. And though biographers gloss over it, the 'world beyond the veil' played a key role in his life. The whole tenor of 'Tam o Shanter' suggests that the events described were ones that Burns himself had experienced. In fact, other poems he wrote were undoubtedly accounts of supernatural visions he had himself been through.

Freemasons have often complained that the key role the organisation played in Burns' life has been played down. Several poems, it is suggested, have themes linked to Freemasonry. One of his most famous poems, 'A Man's a Man for A' That', it has been argued by Masons, expresses everything that Freemasonry stands for. It's also true that as a young man Burns made a serious effort to learn about cosmology, mathematics and surveying – subjects that, it could be argued, had a connection with the Masons. The mysticism linked to Freemasonry clearly played a part in attracting Burns. The contemplation of things beyond everyday life form an important part of the pull of this ancient order, though, as with many organisations, the extent of involvement depended on the attitude of the individual. Exactly how Burns used his time in Freemasonry is still a subject of debate.

Known facts, however, are straightforward. He joined his local Masonic group, the St David's Tarbolton Lodge, on 4 July 1781, located in Tarbolton village. He was twenty-two years old. The fee was twelve shillings and six pence, a considerable sum for a farm worker. In October of that year he passed, as

Freemasonry terms it, to the Fellowcraft degree and was raised to the degree of Master. However, the following year a new lodge was set up, the St James Lodge, also in Tarbolton, which Burns attached himself to. Two years later, in July 1784, Burns was promoted to Deputy Master of the new Lodge. And during his time as a Mason in Ayrshire, Burns used a secret mark as a signature. What it represented and why he used it has been hotly debated. Catherine Smith, in *The Stars of Robert Burns*, argues that it signified a comet which, given the circumstances of his birth and the superstitions surrounding the appearance of these objects in the heavens, sounds plausible. The truth, however, is that no one can be sure what it meant. What may be more significant is that Burns chose to use one at all. Did it form a link to strange visions he had experienced? It seems that by the time he joined the Masons he had been through some unsettling encounters.

There was clearly, however, a strong social aspect to membership of the Freemasons. At a time when social diversions were limited it provided a congenial gathering place where people from different backgrounds who would not normally socialise could get together and interact. So does this explain why people of influence in Ayrshire involved in Freemasonry so readily took up Burns' poetry and set him on the path to stardom? Freemasonry was well established in Scotland, with lodges situated in many areas of the country. There were sixteen in Edinburgh and even five in Dumfries, places which were to play an important role in Burns' life.

But friendship alone, support for a fellow Mason, cannot on its own explain the enthusiasm with which his contacts through the lodge took up his poetry. Nor can it be argued that individuals quite simply immediately recognised his genius as a poet. There was more to it than that. It was, I would suggest, the mystical themes that ran through his verse which proved the attraction. Themes which chimed with the sympathies and outlook of Freemasonry. By the time Burns brought out his collection of poems, *Chiefly in the Scottish Dialect*, the famous Kilmarnock Edition, in the summer of 1786, he had experienced several incidents, including out-of-body experiences, and may even have suffered a nervous breakdown as a result. It has even been suggested that he deliberately chose this time to print his poems as July 1786 was, in astrological terms, a propitious time for someone of his birth date to start out on a new course in life. If so, it certainly worked. But would Burns have taken such matters seriously? We know that in the summer of 1781 Burns fell ill from a mysterious disease which baffled doctors at the time and which has puzzled observers since. He was visited five times in eight days by Dr Charles Fleming, so clearly something had knocked him back. What it was though remains a mystery. And though typical diseases of the period, including smallpox, malaria and typhoid, have been suggested they have all been dismissed as an explanation. A severe mental breakdown, however, has been raised as a possibility. But would it be going too far to suggest that this was a result of his experience with the supernatural?

Burns either directly or through his poetry described a variety of paranormal incidents. He even wrote about astral travel. He described being 'set free from the laws of gravitation which bind us to the globe' and being 'at pleasure to fly free' across the world. In one of his poems included in the Kilmarnock Edition he recounted an out-of-body experience which transported him in June 1786 to the birthday gathering of King George III, and he described what he saw there. But was this something he actively engaged in, or just idle thought? That it might be more than simply imagination is suggested by other incidents, because Burns even claimed to have, at times, the power of second sight, what we know today as remote viewing. He had a vision that his friend Robert Muir was lying badly ill in Edinburgh and as a result made a trip to the capital to see him. He might even also have had his own spirit contact. He had certainly had at least one memorable encounter with a phantom from the other world which he described in his poem 'The Vision'. In it, he relates that while sitting by the fire after a day's work a female figure appeared surrounded by a glowing light. Typical of such strange encounters, as in the Fairy Queen who entranced Thomas the Rhymer, this phantom was clothed in green with holly adorning her head. That this was a representation of the spirit of nature seems clear. She was called Coila, or at least that is what she told Burns her name was. To sceptics, the poem is no more than Burns using his imagination, but taken as an encounter he actually experienced, it shows the extent to which his mind interacted with the enigma of the spirit world and how strongly he felt the supernatural impacted on our own.

It's hard to deny that the mystical aspect of Burns is as key to understanding him as is the political aspect. But it's Burns the revolutionary and patriot that tends to get the press rather than his interest in the supernatural. It should be remembered, however, that Burns was an active Freemason long before he was an active radical. And, it seems reasonable to believe that it was the 'occult Burns' rather than any political aspects which encouraged Freemasons to take up Burns both socially and financially. In truth, it was largely thanks to his contacts in the Lodges that within a six-month period he shot from obscurity to national fame.

The Freemason lodges of the west of Scotland did their best to spread word of their brother poet and, of course, to encourage sales of the Kilmarnock Edition. Burns needed cash to pay the printers and to produce more copies, or even a fresh edition, of his work. He would never have managed this without help. He had already built up through his membership of the St James Lodge in Tarbolton a number of influential contacts, including Professor Dugald Stewart, who was acquainted not only with the local gentry, but the movers and shakers of Edinburgh society. Leading figures of the day were starting to hear the name Robert Burns and were keen to meet the budding poet.

In November 1786, with a growing reputation, Burns travelled to Edinburgh. Here James Dalrymple, a prominent Ayrshire landowner, took him to the Canongate Kilwinning Lodge of Freemasons which could boast an impressive membership of the well-to-do, including a former Lord Advocate, Henry Erskine; the painter Alexander Naysmyth; Lord Torphichen; the judge Lord Elcho and James Cunningham, Earl of Glencairn. Through his contact with Glencairn, Burns struck gold. The Earl persuaded the members of the Caledonian Club, an elite gathering of landed society, to subscribe to a second edition of Burns' poems. His reputation was assured and soon the rich and famous from Inverness to London knew of Burns and his poetry. Within two years his poems were also being published in the United States, and the man from Ayrshire had become a poet with an international reputation.

His most famous poem 'Tam o' Shanter' did not, however, appear till 1790 when he had moved to Dumfriesshire. It was not one, though, that his biographers have tended to dwell on. Brilliantly written as it is, it has the 'unfortunate' theme of the supernatural and seems at odds with the Burns that they would prefer be remembered, the man who dealt with political and patriotic themes. Set against 'A Man's A Man for A' That', 'Tam o' Shanter' can appear almost an aberration, especially as it was during this last part of his life that Burns is seen at his most radical. He even earned a reputation as a

Jacobin, one of the more extreme supporters of the French Revolution which broke out in July 1789. He was spied on by government agents, was forced to publish poetry under assumed names and was reported for treasonable activities.

Why would such a man expend so much effort to produce a poem with the supernatural as its main theme? It can only be because the occult fascinated him and was as important to him as righting the political wrongs of the time. There's no doubt that Burns was passing through a stressful time when he wrote 'Tam o' Shanter'. Success brought recognition, but not financial security, and Burns was forced to look for employment to support his wife and a growing family. A job as an excise man, working for the government, was a solution to his financial problems and Burns was certainly relieved when in August 1789, he was offered the position of Excise Officer to cover Upper Nithsdale in Dumfriesshire at an annual salary of £50.

It was during this period that 'Tam o' Shanter' appeared. However, its origins lay some years earlier when Burns met Francis Grose, a writer and publisher who was travelling round the country researching material for his book *The Antiquities of Scotland*. Burns suggested to Grose that a sketch of the haunted kirk at Alloway be included in his material, which has led to speculation as to why he was so keen that this particular spot be recognised in this way. At the time Burns explained that his interest lay in his own local connection and the fact that his father, William Burns, was buried there. But was there more to it than that? Francis Grose agreed to include the sketch if Burns would provide ghost stories connected with Alloway Kirk. He provided two, one much longer than the first, which Burns claimed he could 'prove'. It was this incident which formed the basis of 'Tam o' Shanter'.

The poem, with its description of an encounter with

witches and demons in Alloway Kirk and a hair-raising chase till running water stops the phantoms in their tracks, is a classic supernatural tale. However, did Burns write it simply to put the graveyard on the map, as some have argued, or because he himself had experienced the spectres he so brilliantly describes? He never admitted it, but the kirk was well known in the area where he was born and brought up as a focus of supernatural activity, the kind of place that Burns was interested in and which aroused his curiosity. There are many unexplained incidents in Burns' life, including a mysterious theft of manuscripts from his lodgings in Edinburgh. He claimed to know the thief but appears to have made no effort to get the papers back or describe what was in them. There's also a suggestion that he 'married' a woman in the Highlands by pagan rights even though he had taken Jean Armour as his wife. But did Burns go as far as to worship pagan deities? His description of visiting standing stone circles, uttering pagan prayers and taking in the rising of the sun at the solstice may or may not be Burns simply in poetic flow. In public, he tended to play down the intensity of his feeling on these matters. But 'Tam o' Shanter' emerged from a real strength of feeling, otherwise it would never have been born.

Burns had a real belief in the afterlife. When his friend Robert Muir lay dying he told him not to be afraid as a new life awaited him. He repeated this theme to one of his main supporters, Mrs Dunlop, on the death of her son in July 1790. Burns was assuredly a Scottish patriot and a political radical, but he was equally a mystic, a man who believed that other worlds were as much a part of our life as our everyday existence.

Charles Edward Stuart,
Bonnie Prince Charlie

Strangely for a radical, but in keeping with a mystic, Burns had a soft spot for the Jacobites. Maybe it was a shared belief in fate. Charles Edward Stuart, Bonnie Prince Charlie, was convinced that he had a date with destiny. To recapture Great Britain for his dynasty after his grandfather had been forced to give up the throne when William of Orange had invaded the country in 1688, the Glorious Revolution. Perhaps, in conscious imitation of Jesus Christ's crusade, he had set out for Scotland on 21 June 1745 aboard the French vessel the *Du Teillay* with exactly twelve followers. Later he would claim he landed in Scotland on 23 July with seven men, seven being long revered by mystics as the most magical of numbers as, to take one instance, the world was created in seven days. And Charles was well aware of the powerful effect the supernatural possessed to encourage his supporters and weaken his enemies.

So did the Jacobite Rising of 1745 fail because the forces of the supernatural turned against Charles? The prince had been brought up in an atmosphere in which the paranormal and mysticism played a key role, or so it was alleged. His grandfather, James II and VII, was believed to possess a magic hat which, like the more usual crystal ball, allowed him to listen to conversations in distant places. It was also said that he had consulted a sorcerer with the aim of sinking the fleet of William of Orange, the man who in 1688 'stole', in James' view, his kingdom from him. His son, James Edward Stuart, Charles' father, was conceived in mystical circumstances following a trip paid by Mary of Modena, wife of James VII, to St Winifred's Well in north Wales, a place long associated with miraculous cures and events. Bonnie Prince Charlie could not easily escape the tradition that the other world looked to his family to return Great Britain to its rightful ruler.

Meanwhile the supporters of William III took every opportunity to sneer at claims that the supernatural world had lined up behind the Jacobites. But was that out of fear and envy rather than disbelief? After James VII's death in 1766 his body, buried in France, became a site of pilgrimage where, it was claimed, miracles took place. The Hanoverians could never match, in Jacobite eyes, the Stuarts' intimacy with the other world, although it was put about that on 6 May 1665 a glowing ball of light had been seen hovering over the Chair of State in Holland, the exact date on which William of Orange became ruler of that country. It could hardly match, however, the Stewarts' long-standing interaction with the world beyond.

However, other incidents could be evidence that not everything would go the Jacobites' way. During the coronation of James VII the state crown, on two separate occasions, almost slipped from his head, an indication to the superstitious that his reign would be a troubled one, as events later proved. When the Old Pretender, James Stewart, raised the standard of revolt at Braemar in 1715, which is itself situated at the head of Glenshee, Glen of the Fairies, his banner, blue in colour – another mystic shade in Scottish folk lore – fell apart. A bad omen for anyone sensitive about the attitude of the other world towards James' venture.

But when Bonnie Prince Charlie approached the Scottish shore in July 1745, the omens appeared far better. As their ship sailed in sight of the Hebrides an eagle, a bird that symbolised royalty, hovered over them. The eagle moved back and forth above the vessel for several hours, a sure sign that the powers above were welcoming a true king back to Scotland. But did that mean that the unseen world was backing the prince? Time would tell.

For the twenty-five-year-old Charles, who had never set foot in Scotland, the country was a land of dreams. A mystical place which, exercising its magic, would transform his fortunes and that of the whole Stewart dynasty. Charles wanted his followers to believe that at last their 'messiah' had arrived and the tide would turn in their favour.

On the other side of Scotland, on 25 July 1745, Duncan Calder an Aberdeenshire seer, glimpsed a vision of the prince landing at Moidart in distant Inverness-shire, as he was, in fact, doing at that very moment. It proved the accuracy of second sight, but being able to see events at a distance or even the future could be a double-edged sword. What if these prophecies revealed the futility of the exercise? For the moment, Charles, excited by the prospects of success, put such doubts to one side.

Other incidents, however, had the prince been aware of them, might have caused him to pause for thought. On the island of Eriskay in the Outer Hebrides, shortly before the prince arrived in Scotland, an unusual event had occurred. Eriskay belonged to Clanranald and the chief of the clan was startled one day to see his hounds chasing an otter, one that was distinctly white in colour. This strange incident was viewed as a bad omen as it was so extraordinary. It meant that something unpleasant was going to happen and that Clanranald would be on the receiving end of the misfortune. Which turned out to be true – punishment, eventually, for supporting the cause of Bonnie Prince Charlie. It's not clear if Clanranald was disconcerted simply by the appearance of the white otter or whether it was because the dogs failed to kill it. Many omens were linked to military expeditions, especially as clans left their own territory and headed for battle. If they ran into an armed man on the way it was viewed as a good omen. However, if they saw a four-legged animal like a deer or fox and failed to kill it then their venture would most likely fail. But the most telling omen of all concerned a woman. And here one can see the survival of pagan belief in the power of the dark goddess. If they met a barefoot woman they would cut her across her forehead with a weapon. The drawing of blood with a metal object would destroy any evil that she might bring down on the clan soldiers.

A prediction made by Cameron of Lochiel followed a similar line, prophesying that the side which first shed blood would be victorious. According to the account, in the ensuing battle at Prestonpans the Jacobites made sure they shot a soldier leading the charge towards them. They were victorious, but whatever magic had been involved did not, unfortunately for Charles Stewart, extend to the whole Jacobite campaign.

Sometimes the shedding of blood as an omen before battle could reach quite horrific peaks. During the 1715 rising, the Highlanders supporting the Old Pretender had allegedly killed one of their opponents and smeared his blood over a standing stone, the White Stone, a prehistoric monument the remains of which can still be seen in a field close to the site of the Battle of Sheriffmuir. The aim was to rouse the magic power within the stone circle and turn it to the advantage of the Jacobite cause. The ensuing battle on 13 November was more or less a drawn one, but, if the magic had not worked on this occasion, it did not discourage the continued use of signs and symbols to both read the future and enlist the support of the mystic world.

In a climate where it was taken for granted that the powers of darkness had to be placated, Charles, understandably, took care to make sure that he countered any events which were seen to weaken the resolve of his army, with its core of clan supporters, to carry on the fight. When in November 1745 he took the fateful step of crossing into England over the

River Esk, an ominous incident occurred. One of his most important followers, Donald Cameron of Lochiel, head of Clan Cameron, cut his hand on his own claymore. It was not seen as a mere accident. It suggested that the army was going to shed its own blood. And a lot of it. Both Charles and Lochiel managed to rally the men forward. But Lochiel's 'accident', coupled with Highland nervousness about crossing a river had unsettled the army. Running water was regarded as a barrier to evil. The River Esk, on the one hand, could be seen as reducing the power of the English, had they invaded Scotland, but once it was crossed in the other direction that mystical barrier was broken and the clansmen would have less protection. So had Lochiel's wound served as a sign that the 'magic' that protected them was from now on weakened? Fanciful? Well, events were certainly to prove the superstitious right, whether by chance or mystical design.

Did Prince Charles worry about those who predicted the doom of his army? Even forecasting the Jacobites' last stand at Culloden? He probably would have chosen to ignore publicly the second sight granted to the unlikely figure of Duncan Forbes, a prominent judge and Lord Advocate. Forbes was a determined enemy of the prince. His mansion, Culloden House, overlooked Drummossie Moor, site of the final confrontation between the two sides. Even as the Jacobites were scoring dramatic victories he predicted that the prince's last hours would be spent at the place which he could clearly see from his study window. It's not clear how he gained this insight, but it seems that he did experience a vision of some kind, one unusual in a normally down-to-earth man.

But Prince Charles could point to other prophecies that suggested he would soon reclaim the throne. And a number of seers even linked the Young Pretender to the ancient druids, that mystical sect from the distant past who worshipped the oak as a sacred tree. It was no coincidence, surely, that the prince's ancestor, Charles II, according to tradition hid in an oak tree following his defeat at the Battle of Worcester and so was saved from being captured. The druids as well were regarded as the followers of the legendary King Arthur in his struggle against the invading Romans. It was put about by the Jacobites, that Arthur's mantle, as the enemy of oppression, had fallen on Bonnie Prince Charlie's shoulders. Even the Bible, it was suggested, backed the Prince. Chapter 38 of the *Book of Ezekiel* described a 'mighty army' coming from the north which would 'attack like a storm and cover the land like a cloud'. And all done with God's blessing.

But to his enemies, Charles was the anti-Christ described in the *Book of Revelation*, the tool of Satanic forces. In fact, to the Hanoverians, the supporters of King William III, the whole Jacobite army was a devilish crew. And the sharply different attitudes held by each side were well displayed in their opposing view of John Graham of Claverhouse, a revered figure to those supporting the return of the Stewart dynasty to the throne. Claverhouse, better known, perhaps as Bonnie Dundee, was a man feared by his enemies not only as a clever general in the cause of James VII, but because, it was said, he had sold his soul to the Devil. His reward came in the form of a horse bred in Hell which could leap any obstacle and clamber any hill. Dundee himself was believed to be invincible to bullets and sword strikes. But could any of this be taken seriously? Especially as Dundee was killed at the moment of his greatest victory, the battle of Killiecrankie in 1689. Of what use was his supposed invincibility then?

There was a suggestion that Dundee had annoyed the fairies by wearing green, the colour they viewed as their own, and so they exacted a deadly vengeance. However, there is no evidence that he wore anything that shade on the fateful day, though the tradition does suggest that his death was seen as a supernatural event. Did even his enemies come to believe that there was something in the supernatural aura that hung over him? Like the folklore linked to vampires and werewolves, it was believed that Dundee could only be brought down by magical means. And so an enterprising soldier, aware that Dundee could not be killed by lead shot, made a bullet from the silver button on his jacket. It was this missile that blasted Dundee's invincibility to smithereens and ended his life. Neither Hanoverians nor Jacobites could entirely dismiss the influence of the supernatural from their actions.

Even illness was used as a tool to rally support. The Stewart kings had regularly put their hands on anyone suffering from scrofula, a disease which causes the glands to swell, as it was believed this would bring about a miraculous cure. George I, who came to the throne in 1714, abandoned the practice. The Jacobites claimed that this was because he did not possess the mystical power to heal. In other words, he was not the true king of Britain. It was a useful piece of propaganda. When George I refused to touch a man's son to heal him, the father took him to the Old Pretender and, after, signed up with the Jacobite army as a result. After Bonnie Prince Charlie performed the ceremony of 'touching' in Perth, it had a similar affect on supporters and encouraged many in the area to join the rising.

Charles' awareness of the supernatural, I would suggest, also explains his decision to wear a blue bonnet and sash when he captured and entered Edinburgh on 17 September 1745, following the Jacobites' triumphant march through Scotland. Blue was a colour associated with the other world, enshrined in the mysterious 'blue blanket' paraded by the citizens of Edinburgh at important events for centuries. It had its origins in the strange tales linking the city, and Scotland, to ancient

Egypt. It's noticeable that when Charles wanted to impress the townspeople of Manchester, he again wore blue. At every town that the Jacobites captured, at the prince's insistence, the blue uniformed cavalrymen of his follower Lord Elcho entered before anyone else. The colour blue clearly had significance for Charles.

In spite of the attempt to enlist the forces of the supernatural and having by December 1745, with little opposition, reached the town of Derby, his main general, Lord George Murray, for reasons that have remained controversial, insisted that the Jacobites end the march on London and withdraw. A long trek back to Scotland followed, soon to be pursued by the Duke of Cumberland, an experienced soldier who was, in fact, Prince Charles' own cousin. A showdown followed at Culloden. A battle Charles insisted on fighting, in spite of warnings about the likely outcome.

There were many bad omens. Alastair Macdonald from Kinloch Rannoch had in the past accidentally killed a government soldier when he threw a gun at him. The gun, thereafter, was seen to have magical powers and became a talisman with the name Gunna Breal. It was passed down the generations and eventually came into the possession of Alexander Macdonald, who used it at the Battle of Prestonpans, a Jacobite victory. Somehow the Gunna Breal warned Alexander that Culloden was going to be a disaster and that he must save the weapon for future generations. He gave it to his servant for safekeeping. The gun hadn't lied and Alexander Macdonald died on Drumossie Moor.

As the opposing armies lined up to face each other on 16 April 1746 nerves were set jangling when a white hare ran through the ranks of the Jacobites then collapsed and died. Charles himself witnessed the incident which he regarded as a bad omen for the battle. He was also aware that a skree, a strange mythical creature part human and part bird, had been seen hovering over the Jacobite army the night before the battle. By tradition, it was a harbinger of doom and certainly weakened the resolve of the superstitious of whom there were many in his army.

After the disaster of the defeat, some blamed Lord George Murray. He should, perhaps, have taken the influence of superstition more seriously. In the dispositions of the army at Culloden he placed the Atholl men on the right wing of the army, a place normally held by the Macdonalds, as they pointed out they had held that position in every major battle where they had fought since Bannockburn in 1314. There's no doubt that Murray's decision was seen as ominous which, as things began to go wrong, preyed on the minds of the Macdonald men and undermined their morale at key points in the fight.

Tales of the use of magic during the final showdown at Culloden abound. One Macdonald chief from Skye had a charm placed on his jacket by a seer on the island. By the power of the other world no bullets could now penetrate it, even though during the battle he was peppered with Redcoat shot. As defeat overtook the Jacobites, Macdonald fled the battlefield throwing away his coat to escape more easily. Tradition has it that when it was later found it was full of gunshot holes, but somehow not a mark had been left on Macdonald's body.

Charles' defeat at Culloden ended the Stewart cause and the prince was forced, after months of hiding from government forces, to return to France. He lived on till 1788, dying aged sixty-eight, in Rome. He never returned to Scotland. But, in supernatural terms, he lived on. The prince had left a mystical trail wherever he went. On the run in Skye with Flora Macdonald he ran into a newly married couple, Mr and Mrs

Beaton, who offered the fugitives a drink of milk. When Mrs Beaton bore a child nine months later it was said that the features of Prince Charles had impressed themselves on the features of the baby.

To supporters, the prince radiated a supernatural aura. Sheets he slept in while on Skye were kept and used as a winding sheet and later wrapped the corpse of Flora Macdonald; the ones on the bed he occupied in Elgin were used by Lady Arradoul as a shroud. And the link between the Jacobites and the supernatural refuses to die. As recently as the year 2000, the ghost of Jean Cameron, a fanatical supporter of Prince Charles who was present when he raised his standard at Glenfinnan in August 1745 and followed him on his campaign, was alleged to haunt the streets of East Kilbride. Following Charles' defeat, she moved to the area but expressed a dying wish to be buried in the Highlands at Lochaber, a key area of Jacobite support. Her request was never carried out, so her spirit walks the plains of the Lowlands. Even in death, it seems, Jean wished to be close to a cause which meant so much to her and for which so many died in vain.

James Hogg, the Ettrick Shepherd

Bonnie Prince Charlie may have seen the supernatural as no more than a useful tool in his campaign, but to others the unseen world was up close and personal. James Hogg, the Ettrick Shepherd, a poet and novelist, was a man obsessed with the paranormal. In later life he claimed that his birth in November 1770 was marked by strange signs and portents: a bogle, a goblin of the Scottish Borders, was known to haunt the area where he was born and screamed out at the moment of Hogg's arrival into the world. Oddly, Hogg would tell his

James Hogg

friends that he was born on 25 January, the anniversary of Robert Burns' birth, though this was quite simply untrue. He was a man, as his writings would show, who seemed to inhabit two worlds at one and the same time. Phantoms and strange beings of every kind interacted with Hogg's everyday existence so that even he admitted at times he could not separate reality from the world of dreams.

He certainly came from a background steeped in the supernatural. His mother, Margaret Laidlaw, was a 'wise woman', one who could see ahead in time and recognise the signs from the other world not visible to most people. Involvement with the paranormal was a Laidlaw family tradition stretching into the mists of the past. There was a well-known legend that in the thirteenth century an ancestor of Margaret's had fought a psychic duel with Michael Scott, one of Scotland's most famous, or notorious, magicians. Hogg might even have visited the spot where this encounter took place – Michael Scott's castle at Aikwood was close to the place where he was brought up and still visible as a ruin.

More disturbing was the tale that in the sixteenth century another of Hogg's ancestors had been a notorious witch who had been taken to task by her husband, a Laidlaw, for practising the black arts. In response, she cursed the Laidlaw family, prophesying that they would prosper for nine generations, but fall into poverty thereafter. It's not clear whether Hogg took this curse seriously, although his father Robert, a tenant farmer did become bankrupt, and from comparative wealth, Hogg was forced at an early age to take to the hills as a shepherd. Poverty undoubtedly dogged him all through his life, and he never achieved the income enjoyed by his friend and contemporary Sir Walter Scott.

But that was in the future. His early years were filled with tales and legends of the supernatural poured in his ear by his mother who apparently revelled in her reputation as one with second sight. As a teenager wandering the hills of his neighbourhood, watching over flocks of sheep, Hogg heard story after story from other herdsmen of encounters with fairies, phantoms, brownies and even weirder spectres of the dark.

Hogg soon had terrifying experiences of his own to recount. When he was nineteen, he was out walking through a mist one day and was suddenly surrounded by a bright light. He saw a figure that frightened him so much that at first he thought he had encountered the Devil. The following day the phantom appeared to him again as a 'blackamoor', a dark-complexioned person, as the Devil in classic witchcraft trials was often described. In later years, Hogg wrote that what he had seen had been an apparition of himself, but quite what he meant by that is open to debate. This was certainly not a one-off event.

In the summer he had an equally strange experience. As he was walking through farmland, he glanced across a nearby burn and saw a herd of Highland cattle being driven down a local drove road. It looked so real that Hogg called for help from other shepherds to move the intruders out of their fields before all the pasture was demolished. But the herd suddenly disappeared, leaving Hogg wondering about the vision he had witnessed. It may be that Hogg had inherited second sight from his mother and suspected as much. However, as a man with literary ambitions and a wish to be taken seriously as a writer, it would be risky to admit as much at a time when belief in the supernatural was regarded as out of date and irrational.

That Hogg may have been witnessing scenes from other worlds or places is given some support by other odd incidents he described. On one occasion, in a snowstorm, he had a vision of a huge forest of trees stretching for mile after mile far into the distance. Once again, his explanation for this incident is puzzling, as he appears to both describe it as something strange and otherworldy but downplay it as having a rational basis. However, it's hard to escape the conclusion that Hogg saw the body as having a spirit form which could, on occasion, free itself and drift away. He tells how in December 1798 as a twenty-eight-year-old, he fell seriously ill. During his sickness the woman watching over him saw a wraith appear, a being that takes the soul as it leaves the body. Its appearance suggested that Hogg was at death's door. He recovered, however, but the incident intrigued him. And following it, Hogg often visited a place close to the Borders town of Selkirk, known as Fauldhouse, where the spirits of the dead were said to gather. He never admitted to encountering any phantoms there, but he was a man who went from one extreme to another. Describing the most bizarre incidents, engaging in odd behaviour, but on the other hand appearing at times almost meek, placid and downright traditional. He veered from outright belief in the supernatural to, at times, outright scepticism. In a way, he reflected the mood of the times.

James Hogg was born in a but and ben farmhouse at Ettrickhall in Selkirkshire, close to Ettrick parish church. The nearest towns were Selkirk, about sixteen miles distant, and Moffat, nineteen miles away. At the time it was a remote spot among the hills, but attractive to farmers. Hogg, without an independent income, had no choice but to make his own way in the world, though as it turned out he was not a successful businessman and several attempts to set up his own farm failed. Yet even as a teenager Hogg had literary aspirations. His first published poem, 'The Mistake of the Night', appeared in the *Scots Magazine* in 1794 when he was only twenty-four. However, it was the publication in 1797 of Burns' 'Tam o' Shanter', with its key themes of the supernatural and local legends, that inspired him. These were topics close to his own heart. From then till his death in 1835, works of all kinds poured from Hogg's pen – plays, poems and prose works. He had to fight for recognition, but by the 1820s he was being published in the best-known magazines in both Edinburgh and London. His poems and novels were circulating abroad and he had gained an international reputation.

Unfortunately for Hogg, though, he was eclipsed in his lifetime by the genius of Sir Walter Scott. Two centuries on, however, whilst Scott's stock has fallen from admittedly dizzy heights, Hogg's reputation has risen. His best-known work, *The Private Confessions and Memoirs of a Justified Sinner*, published in 1824 and poorly received at the time, has worn much better than Sir Walter's historical novels. Its theme of psychological conflict, the divided self, and its supernatural overtones are more in tune with today's feelings than the Wizard of the North's prodigious output. Hogg, who clearly resented his friend's greater reputation, would no doubt have been delighted.

But perhaps he had only himself to blame if his contemporaries looked at him askance. He undeniably put out some weird stories about himself, even suggesting at one time that he had engaged in cannibalism. He certainly appeared obsessed with the idea. In 1825 he published a poem, 'The Gruesome Caryl', in which a party of soldiers search out a cannibal who is terrorising the area where Hogg lived. They track the human beast to a cave where they discover several women and children who the ogre had intended to feast on. In another poem, 'The Lord of Balloch', a chef is taken captive and, to save himself, attempts to cook his own flesh. Then again in his 'Tales of the Wars of Montrose', Hogg describes lovingly and gruesomely the smell of roasting human flesh as a meal is being prepared. He even wrote in 1823 in *Blackwood's* magazine that he had been 'fed upon flesh', by which he meant both human and animal meat. It was an odd thing to write, and if it was meant to shock, it achieved its purpose, though it hardly enhanced his literary reputation.

Hogg also claimed some strange abilities, writing that he could read a person's mind, and even become that person simply by aping their manner, posture and features. Was this something he had learnt from his mother Margaret Laidlaw? Like her he had a fixation with the threat from witchcraft, a fear which he covered in poems and novels. In his book *The Three Perils of Man*, published in 1822, he defined two of the perils as woman and witchcraft. It was generally believed that the female sex was more likely to fall under the influence of Satan and become involved in black magic. Did he have his mother in mind? In his short work 'The Witch of Fife' Hogg relates the tale of a man who discovers that his wife is a practising witch. It turns out that at night she mounts a Satanic horse which flies her to far-flung and mystic lands where she engages in sex with warlocks. Her husband asks her if he can come too, but she refuses to let him join in. The tales he had heard from his mother and the many stories he had listened to – all allegedly true according to the witnesses – and his own experiences must certainly have had an impact. After Hogg's death, his daughter, Mary Garden, admitted that her father believed both in ghosts and demonic possession. To that might be added the influence and pervasiveness of witchcraft.

One reason for Hogg's better appreciation in the twenty-first century may be that the supernatural themes he dealt with – out-of-body experiences, coupled with assistance from angels, and in addition, alien encounters – have a contemporary resonance. In the poem 'The Pilgrims of the Sun', a young woman's astral spirit travels though the solar system, accompanied by a strange being called Cela. On their journey they visit both the planets Mars and Venus. The similarity of this account to the alien abduction reports of the 1950s is uncanny. Did Hogg himself experience something other worldly? He also published, in 1830, 'Dr David Dale's Account of a Grand Aerial Voyage', a story of a journey two Scots make to the moon and back.

It might be thought that respectable society would have steered clear of James Hogg. Far from it. Less well known is the fact that Hogg wrote and had published many articles on political subjects. Only recently has the academic world started to explore the influence Hogg exerted in the area of politics, and there seems little doubt that there is much to be revealed. It's hard to imagine that the Tory party in the class-ridden era of the 1820s and 1830s would finance a man like James Hogg with his obsession with witchcraft, magic and all the elements that make up the supernatural, but that is exactly what happened. Robert Peel, later Prime Minister, sent Hogg a personal letter of gratitude, enclosing his own cheque for £100. Later he sent an additional £40, which he intended to turn into an annual pension, but was prevented from doing so when the Tories were turned out of office. It's hard to believe that this was done simply out of concern for Hogg's financial situation. The truth was that the Ettrick Shepherd had been campaigning determinedly for the Tory party, writing articles for key Tory supporting publications including *Fraser's Magazine*, *Blackwood's* and *The Royal Lady's Magazine*.

Hogg's attraction to Toryism appears strange and out of character at first glance; however, it chimes with his fear that the stability of society was under threat, both at the day-to-day level from radical forces, and on the psychic level from the dark entities inhabiting the other worlds invisible to most folk. When Hogg visited London in December 1830 it was not purely a social visit. He met several members of parliament, including Sir John Malcolm and Sir George Warrender. He attended debates at the House of Commons, dined with Macleod of Macleod and was invited to the exclusive Society of Beefsteaks by Lord Saltoun. Membership was limited to twenty-four, and even the King was in the queue to join. So highly regarded was Hogg that when he was invited to dinner with the Duke of Sussex, the King's brother, it was rumoured that, as with Walter Scott, he was about to receive a knighthood. It did not come about, as it turned out, but that may have been due more to the declining influence of the Tory party than anything else. Why Hogg, with his bizarre tales of cannibalism, witchcraft, encounters with strange entities and supernatural beings, should be so popular with the London upper class is a mystery.

He was undeniably a member of a number of odd societies that may have had links to similar clubs in the south. There was the Bowmen of the Border, founded by Hogg, which dressed in Lincoln green and associated with the legendary Robin Hood. The connection with pagan worship and the spirits of the forest are well established, though it's unclear whether any of that was involved in Hogg's brainchild. The Dilettanti Club, of which Hogg was a founding member in 1809, has been seen as a successor to the more notorious Hellfire Clubs of the eighteenth century, which undoubtedly had included leading politicians in its membership and pagan rites in its rituals. Evidence in the case of the Dilettanti Club, however, is simply lacking. Exactly why Hogg was so in favour with metropolitan society remains obscure.

His coverage of the weird and wonderful clearly, though, struck a chord, which may explain why in the last few months of his life the prestigious Canongate Kilwinning Lodge in Edinburgh invited him to join the Freemasons. Hogg was too ill to attend and take part in the ritual membership process.

He did, however, accept the honour of becoming the Lodge's poet laureate in succession to Robert Burns. Hogg, ambitious to the last, was thrilled.

Hugh Miller

It's strange how reputations come and go. Today the name Hugh Miller probably doesn't bring instant recognition, but in his day during the nineteenth century, he was one of the most famous Scots of his generation. His place in history rests on the role he played in founding and developing the scientific investigation of the earth's crust, known today as geology. Sir Archibald Geikie, a fellow Scot who also made a huge contribution to the then new science, wrote of Hugh Miller that during his lifetime and for some years afterwards, he was regarded by his countrymen as the leading geologist of his day. And this estimate spread even more extensively in the United States. On both sides of the Atlantic, ideas of the nature and scope of geology were largely drawn from him.

What is even more remarkable about Hugh Miller is that he was self taught and did not have the advantage of most of those involved in scientific investigation of benefitting from a university education. Furthermore, his interest in the sciences was only one aspect of a varied life. He edited a leading Scottish newspaper, assisted in the foundation of the Free Church of Scotland, engaged in a literary battle with supporters of evolution and wrote articles on every conceivable subject. A book of his essays published in 1870 after his death included pieces on the Scott Monument, the sanctities of matter, the *Encyclopaedia Britannica*, a vision of the railroad and, to show that, as the French put it, 'the more things change, the more they're the same', one titled 'The Conclusion of the War in

Afghanistan'. In an age when specialisation and detailed knowledge of one area was the trend, Hugh Miller bucked it. He had an interest in every activity that the world engaged in.

But scientists have never forgiven him for one thing which may help to explain why his reputation has descended from the heights: his obsession with the supernatural. Hugh Miller is a classic example of how the struggle between science and the paranormal can be played out in one man's life, and perhaps how the forces of the supernatural finally destroyed one of the greatest minds of the time. But were images of the worlds beyond no more than the phantoms circulating inside Hugh's head? There can be little doubt that, fascinated as he became by scientific investigation, Hugh Miller was constantly grappling with the pull that the supernatural exercised on his thoughts. It had started at an early age in the house in Cromarty where he was born on 10 October 1802, a cottage that had been built by his great-grandfather John Feddes who, according to family tradition, had made his fortune as a buccaneer in the Caribbean. As Hugh described it in his autobiography, *My Schools and Schoolmasters*:

One day when playing all alone at the stair foot – for the inmates of the house had gone out – something extraordinary had caught my eye on the landing place above and looking up, there stood John Feddes – for I somehow instinctively divined that it was none other than he – in the form of a large, tall, very old man, attired in a light blue greatcoat. He seemed to be steadfastly regarding me with apparent complacency, but I was sadly frightened and for years after when passing through the dingy, ill-lighted room out of which I had inferred he had come, I used to feel not at all sure that I might not tilt against old John in the dark.

87

This encounter predates the incident more often referred to by writers, the strange event that occurred on the death of his father, a ship's captain, when Hugh was only five. He recounted it in his book *Scenes and Legends of Northern Scotland*, published in 1835:

There were no forebodings in our house for a letter [from his father] had just been received. My mother was sitting on the evening after, beside the fire, plying the cheerful needle, when the house door, which had been left unfastened, fell open, and I was despatched from her side to shut it. Day had not wholly disappeared, but it was fast posting on to night, and a grey haze spread a neutral tint of dimness over every more distant object, but left the nearer ones comparatively distinct, when I saw at the open door within less than a yard of my breast, as plainly as ever I saw anything, a dissevered hand and arm stretched towards me. Hand and arm were apparently those of a female; they bore a livid and sodden experience; and directly fronting me, where the body ought to have been, there was only blank, transparent space, through which I could see the dim forms of the objects beyond. I was fearfully startled and ran shrieking to my mother, telling what I had seen; and the house-girl whom she next sent to shut the door, apparently affected by my terror, also returned frightened and said that she too had seen the woman's hand . . . my mother going to the door saw nothing, though she appeared much impressed by the extremeness of my terror and the minuteness of my description.

Soon after Hugh learned that his father had drowned around the same time that he had witnessed the disembodied arm. These two incidents, both of which took place at an early age, haunted him throughout his life, as they provoked in his mind a confrontation, the reality embodied within the world of science, against those phantoms of the night which science proclaimed could simply not exist.

By the 1850s Miller had achieved a great deal and should have been a contented man. His writings on geology had spread across the world. His collection of fossils, many of them dug up from the area round Cromarty, was recognised as one of the most influential in helping to reconstruct the earth's geological past. They could be found on display at many venues, including the prestigious British Museum. One fossilised fish, *pterichthys milleri*, was even named in his honour. He was well known to most of the famous names of the time and in contact with many of them, including Andrew Carnegie, the millionaire industrialist, and John Muir, the founder of environmentalism. His views on a range of subjects, not only geology but particularly on the relationship, in the era before Darwin, between evolution and the Bible, were widely read and taken seriously.

At a family level, he was happily married to Lydia, an authoress in her own right, who had borne him four children. Living in Edinburgh and much admired, he had left his less prosperous life in Cromarty, where he had trained as a stonemason, to a comparative life of ease in the capital. Why then did events take such a tragic turn? Were demons quite literally intent on destroying his mind?

Miller's first residence in Edinburgh had been a house he had rented at 5 Sylvan Place in the Sciennes district bordering the Meadows. From there it was a short walk to his offices at the *Witness* newspaper, which he edited. In April 1854, however, as his finances had considerably improved, he bought a house in Portobello – Shrub Mount – which stood on the

89

shore side of the High Street. At the time it was described as 'an eighteenth-century cottage with its own grounds'. It was in this idyllic setting with everything to live for that Hugh Miller killed himself. It was an act that puzzled friends and family at the time and has aroused controversy ever since. Did Hugh Miller really believe he was under assault by elements of the paranormal?

There's general agreement about the immediate circumstances which led up to his death. On 23 December 1856 Miller, as was his custom, helped his daughter with her school homework. Having completed that task he picked up a book of poems by William Cowper and, like a traditional Victorian parent, read several poems out loud to his children. As a public figure he received many letters each day from all manner of correspondents. He liked to deal with these in the evening after the children had gone to bed, so bidding them goodnight he headed for his study where he spent some time working. It's unclear exactly what he dealt with on this particular night, but having finished he retired to his bedroom next door to rest. It was a routine that he followed every day like clockwork, and there was no warning of what was to follow.

At some hour during the night, Hugh Miller returned to his study, took off the fisherman's jersey he was wearing, and, having put a handgun to his chest, pulled the trigger to send a bullet through his body. It seems he died instantly. No one heard him cry out or, apparently, the sound of the weapon being fired. We know that because, in spite of several people – his wife and children – being asleep in Shrub Mount, no one was woken by the explosion, and Hugh's corpse remained undiscovered till the following morning. It was found by Lydia, who claimed that she immediately guessed that it had been a tragic mishap, assuming that he had been fiddling with a loaded gun and it had gone off accidentally. Curiously, she missed the suicide note he had left on his desk, which was only discovered by the Reverend Thomas Guthrie, who had arrived to console Lydia as news of Hugh's death spread. How it had been overlooked is another puzzle entwined in these enigmatic events.

The note from Hugh to his wife read:

> Dearest Lydia,
> My brain burns. I *must* have *walked*; and a fearful dream rises upon me. I cannot bear the horrible thought. God and father of the Lord Jesus Christ, have mercy on me. Dearest Lydia, dear children farewell. My brain burns as the recollection grows. My dear, dear wife, farewell.
> Hugh Miller

It undoubtedly sounded like a suicide note, but what had driven Miller to commit such an act? And what did the content of his last message mean? It wasn't obvious to anyone. It appeared an odd death for a man of science and of God. On the surface, he seemed to have a lot to live for, his reputation was high, he was in regular demand as a speaker and writer. A post-mortem added little to the fact of his death. It declared that Hugh's brain had a diseased appearance and that he had taken his own life while temporarily insane. The disease, however, was not specified nor was the connection to the temporary insanity. It struck many as a bit of gloss to smooth over the many unanswered questions over the circumstances of his death.

No one wanted to admit that a famous man of science had been scared into oblivion by the phantoms and spectres of other worlds. But there is evidence that the demonic presence was preying on Miller's mind in the weeks leading up to his suicide. Lydia, in her later biography of her husband, blamed

Hugh's mother for filling his mind with tales of demons and other evil creatures. She wrote that these stories had the effect of depressing his spirits. But if all he had ever experienced were the legends told to him in his childhood, it's hard to believe that this alone would have tipped him over the edge. There was clearly more to it than that.

Shortly before his death, two things appeared to be worrying him. One was the fate of his fossil collection. He claimed that he was concerned that it might be stolen. It was for this reason that he bought a gun, he said. At the same time he told friends that he was nervous about his garden at Shrub Mount being invaded and the house being entered. They assumed he was talking about criminal activity, but it was just at this time that Miller felt that his mind was being assaulted by beings from the world beyond. And this may explain those otherwise enigmatic words in his suicide letter, 'I *mus. have walked;* and a fearful dream rises upon me. I cannot bear the horrible thought.'

Perhaps Lydia had a point in laying the blame on Hugh's mother for sparking his interest in the supernatural. But that hardly explains a fascination that runs through his best-known works, *Scenes and Legends of the North of Scotland* and *My Schools and Schoolmasters*. His obsession surely had a far deeper basis. His childhood encounters with phantoms had certainly caught his imagination, as he himself had documented, but as an adult, he could have left that behind him. Instead he made it a point to record the many legends and bizarre incidents he came across. One in particular provides, I believe, a clue to his view of the supernatural and its interaction with our own world. He recorded it in *My Schools and Schoolmasters*, claiming that it was an account told to him by a relative. However, I'd suggest that this was another strange incident that Miller himself either experienced or witnessed directly, as it comes over so vividly. It was George, his cousin who, wrote Miller, told him of the 'Celtic theory of dreaming, of which I have since often thought'.

It was a bizarre story. According to the account given by Hugh:

Two young men had been spending a summer day in exactly such a scene as that in which he communicated the anecdote to me. There was an ancient ruin beside them, separated, however, from the mossy bank on which they sat by a slender stream, across which there lay a few withered grass stalks. Overcome by the heat of the day, one of the young men fell asleep; his companion watched drowsily beside him, when all at once the watcher was aroused to attention by seeing a little indistinct form, scarce larger than a bee, issue from the mouth of the sleeping man and leaping upon the moss, move downwards to the stream which it then crossed along the withered grass stalks and disappeared amid the nooks and crevices of the ruin. Alarmed by what he saw, the watcher hastily shook his companion by the shoulder and woke him, though with all his haste, the little cloud-like creature, still more rapid in its movements, issued from the crevices into which it had gone, and flying across the stream, instead of creeping along the grass stalks as before, it re-entered the mouth of the sleeper, just as he was in the act of awakening.

The man from whose mouth the creature had emerged then explained what he had experienced as he slept:

I dreamt I was walking through a fine country, and came at length to the shores of a noble river; and just where the clear water went thundering down a precipice

93

there was a bridge all of silver, which I crossed, and then entering a noble palace on the opposite side, I saw great heaps of gold and jewels, and I was just going to load myself with treasure when you rudely awoke me and I lost all.

Miller ends the story in a manner that suggests that he believed this incident was much more than a figment of the imagination. 'I know not what', he added, 'asserters of the clairvoyant faculty may think of the story, but I rather believe that I have occasionally seen them make use of anecdotes that did not rest on evidence a great deal more solid than this Highland legend'. In other words, this event was as worthy of being taken seriously as any encounter that pointed to the existence of strange, other-worldly entities.

I'd suggest that it was accounts like this, especially where it involved direct interaction with the enchanted lands, which not only intrigued but worried Miller. His desperate last words, 'I *must* have *walked*; and a fearful dream rises upon me', suggest that he believed that he himself had been wandering through the lands of Celtic legend, but not encountering a world of wonder. Instead he found himself plagued by phantoms of the demonic sort till his mind could no longer cope with the impact of these dreadful visions.

In another description of the legends of the countryside of his birth, Miller wrote of the goblin of the streams and rivers which 'took malignant delight in luring into its pools, or overpowering in its fords, the benighted traveller. This water-wraith used to appear as a tall woman dressed in green, who used to start, it was said, out of the river before the terrified traveller, to beckon him invitingly on'. In a sentence which sums up both his fears and doubts about the supernatural he closes by saying that when swimming 'at sunset over some dark pool, where the eye failed to mark or the foot to sound the distant bottom, the twig of some sunken bush or tree has struck against me as I passed, I have felt, with a sudden start, as if touched by the cold, bloodless fingers of the goblin'.

Man of science that he was, Miller could still never escape the sense that there were beings and lands beyond the borders of our own reality. If it was all in his imagination, as some would have us believe, then it was a vision of his own creation that drove him to his death. On the other hand, perhaps Hugh Miller had genuinely glimpsed a threat to his very soul and decided on the ultimate, drastic remedy. The supernatural had triumphed over science.

Sir Walter Scott

Phantoms of the night, however, don't seem to have troubled Scotland's greatest writer, Sir Walter Scott. In fact, he gave the impression of feeling quite at home with them. Perhaps that explains a curious incident recorded after his death. The horses pulling his funeral cortege to his burial place at Dryburgh Abbey stopped suddenly and refused to move. This spot, with its magnificent view of the Eildon Hills, has ever since been known as Scott's View. There are those who doubt that this event ever happened, but whether real or myth, it typifies a key aspect of Scott's life: his fascination with and involvement in the supernatural.

In his lifetime, Walter Scott was the most famous writer of his time, not only in Britain but across the world. For a proposed biography of Napoleon, which ran to nine volumes, he received the huge advance, in today's value, of £400,000. His yearly earnings ran to several hundred thousand pounds. His influence was immense. In one year alone 'The Lady of the Lake' (1810) sold over 30,000 copies and sparked a tourist invasion of the Trossachs. It also inspired the US presidential greeting 'hail to the Chief'. Mark Twain even claimed that Scott was partially responsible for starting the American Civil War because he encouraged, with books like *Ivanhoe* and *The Talisman*, the southern plantation owners to adopt a romantic view of themselves quite at odds with their cousins in the go-getting north. On top of that he arranged the visit of George IV to Edinburgh in 1822, prompted the discovery of the Scottish crown jewels, and was offered but turned down the post of poet laureate. As Sir Walter lay dying in 1832, daily bulletins were issued on the state of his health. He was without a doubt Scotland's uncrowned king of that time. But did he have a darker side? His interest in the supernatural and occult is uncontested. He published the well-known *Letters on Demonology and Witchcraft*, a collection of reports of paranormal events, mainly in the Borders, that was for many years a staple source for those investigating the supernatural. This, however, did not appear till 1830, towards the end of his life, although it does show that his interest in occult matters continued right up to the very last.

His novels, however, are full of references to the weird and bizarre. Ghosts, spirits, haunted rooms and castles, witches, fairies, men with second sight and more appear at one time or another in almost every book that he wrote. So was the man who produced such classic works as *Waverley*, *Rob Roy*, and *Ivanhoe* simply playing out an obsession with the supernatural, or was there more to it than that?

Even Sir Walter's admirers admit that there was something odd about the man. Abbotsford, the home he bought in 1811 in his beloved Borders, startled visitors. It was here that Scott liked to display the weird collection of objects that he had gathered, including a preserved calf's heart pierced by pins, a spell used in witchcraft, a painting of the severed head of Mary Queen of Scots, various instruments of torture, adder stones with magical powers, rings said to have once been owned by fairies, and a host of items connected to the supernatural. Scott felt quite at home with his bizarre assortment. He was avidly collecting by his early twenties and employed a range of contacts to supply him with any object that they believed would be weird enough to attract his interest.

But why did Scott choose to move to Abbotsford in the first place? He was born in Edinburgh on 5 August 1771. His father was a lawyer and his mother the daughter of a professor of medicine. He did have connections with the Borders. His grandfather owned a farm there, Sandyknowe, and aged five Scott was sent there to recover after contracting infantile polio which left him with a permanent lameness in his leg. Here, Scott later claimed, a nursemaid tried to kill him with a pair of scissors believing him to be possessed by the Devil. It's said that she was unhinged by an illegitimate pregnancy, though the facts aren't clear and having a child while not married was a common occurrence of the time. It was during this period that Sir Walter's interest in the supernatural events that were part and parcel of Border's life was first aroused. It became an obsession. In adulthood he was well known to have the most extensive collection of books on all aspects of the occult. One friend wrote to him, sending a book on astrology he had bought in Paris while another jokingly reprimanded him for buying up every book available on witchcraft so that he had no opportunity to build up his own library on the subject.

Scott, in fact, chose the site of Abbotsford for a good reason. He was fascinated by the Tale of Thomas the Rhymer and his encounter with the phantoms of another world. He wanted to be close to and even own that very spot at Huntly Bank where, according to tradition, Thomas had encountered the green clothed Queen of Fairyland, and possess too the aptly-named Bogle Burn along the side of which she reputedly rode. He would take visitors on a tour of these 'magic' spots and even built steps to the site known as the Rhymer's Waterfall so that he could reach it more easily. What's even odder, however, is that the location of the site of Thomas's encounter is disputed and may, in fact, be located a few miles from where Scott claimed it was. It's hard to believe that Scott was not well aware of this. It shows how intense his urge was to be linked to this mystical event, that he was prepared to twist the facts and relocate the incident to Abbotsford to suit his own purpose.

In 1818 he bought land next to Cauldshiel's Loch, home to a mystic water bull, a supernatural beast that occasionally appeared and could be heard roaring to announce its presence. Scott told the American writer Washington Irving that a man he was acquainted with had seen it, and Irving had the impression that Scott believed the event had taken place. One might doubt it had Sir Walter not recorded strange events that he had personally been involved in and seemed to have accepted that what had happened to him had been real. And should it so readily be accepted that Scott's interest in these matters was no more than that of the casual observer? That he regarded the supernatural as no more than a curiosity and did not believe in its reality? Or did Scott practice what he taught and wrote? Did he take his interest in the occult beyond the stage of simply reading and collecting to testing the reality of other worlds?

On the face of it, Sir Walter appears a straightforward character. His fall in the 1820s into catastrophic debt suggests a certain naivety. His determination to pay it off, working himself to death in doing so, suggests a person of honour. But he was certainly also capable of leading a double life and going to extraordinary lengths to do so. For years, for reasons which strike most people as bizarre, he refused to admit to being the author of his most famous books and went to extreme efforts to hide his involvement, even writing critical reviews of his works in order to conceal the connection. His manuscripts were secretly copied and proof corrections carried out in the actual place of printing so that no one had a chance to recognise his handwriting. Other complicated measures were put in place, all aimed at distancing Sir Walter from his novels so that the writing of these world-famous books that were earning vast sums of money could never be laid at his door. Scott's behaviour continues to puzzle. Why was he so determined to lead this double life? What was he trying to hide?

His eventual explanation does not clear up the mystery. In fact, it adds to it. The occasion he chose to make his admission to being the author of the *Waverley* novels might at first seem odd. After all, Scott in 1827 was one of the most famous people on the planet. Anything he said would immediately be spread over newspapers across the world and be the gossip from aristocratic drawing rooms to the common tavern. Revealing his authorship would be an automatic sensation, so why did he pick a dinner being held for the Edinburgh Theatrical Fund on 23 February 1827 as the event at which to own up? But maybe it does make a weird kind of sense, though Scott certainly made it sound strange by the explanation he used for his concealment. Theatres are all about illusion, pretence and fantasy masquerading as reality. Is this what Scott meant about his life, that people only saw his image, they did not see the real person? If so, then the comparison Scott used to explain himself strikes one as unnerving.

He used the example of Arlecchino, better known as Harlequin, with his diamond-covered costume and black mask, to account for his deception, saying that, 'The mask was essential to the performance of the character'. It might be asked why it was so necessary as there was nothing outrageous in the novels themselves. Or was there? Did Scott believe that the appearance of so much that was occult and supernatural in the works revealed more about himself than he wanted to admit to? The image he used of Harlequin in his 'confession' speech was odd. Harlequin evolved out of the more sinister Hellquin, a character who in legend led an army of demons whose purpose was to tour the land seeking evil people whose souls would then be dragged down to Hell. It's hard to believe that Scott picked this particular example by chance. Did he mean that he himself had encountered some dreadful evil or experienced a paranormal encounter of some kind that forced him to distance himself from his own books? Did he believe that he had entered into a pact with the supernatural of some kind?

On the face of it, it seems unlikely, but his fascination with the occult and his strange double life suggests that there is a link here of some kind. And Scott originally had no intention of revealing his authorship during his lifetime. It was financial ruin that eventually forced him out into the open. The plan was that the original manuscripts in his own writing, released only after his death, would tell the tale. Perhaps there was other evidence that might have emerged with these writings, but Sir Walter's image was quickly brushed up by John Lockhart's seven-volume biography of his father-in-law, published in 1837, which, as the standard work, led the way for the sanitised picture of the man we have today. However, even Lockhart and those who followed have been unable to wholly gloss over the fact that Scott was a far stranger character than appears at first glance. Lockhart had to admit that Scott let his mind 'run wild about ghosts and witches and horoscopes'.

His interest in witchcraft was all consuming and lasted a lifetime. Scott possessed three charms against evil. One was a flat, heart-shaped, dark-coloured stone that could be hung round the neck. It was supposed to be especially powerful in protecting women giving birth and to counter acts of witchcraft. Babies were believed to be particularly susceptible to the effects of sorcery. It is likely that Sir Walter's wife, Charlotte Carpenter, who he married in 1797, wore it. They had four children, and childbirth would be an appropriate time to make use of it. Charlotte also owned a magic charm, a set of amber beads given to her by Scott after their marriage, which according to one of her servants she valued for its power to ward off evil forces. Scott had also collected his second charm, a toadstone, which as the name suggests, was a stone found in the head of a toad and so possessed of magic to protect whoever wore it against demons and other malign spirits. Then there was the charm against witches, a lump of clay-like substance imbued with magic power that Scott preserved in a jar.

But were these no more than curiosities, or did Scott take them at face value? He certainly believed that he had encountered spirits from other worlds. When he was staying at his home at Ashiestiel near Selkirk sometime between 1804 and 1812, he saw in the distance an apparition, a woman dressed in brown. He was on horseback and rode towards it, but when he arrived at the spot it had vanished. He turned round and saw that the phantom was now about fifty yards behind him. He tried to reach it, but again it vanished then reappeared at a distance from him. Sir Walter took it as a warning that something evil was about to happen, though he never confirmed if it turned out to be the case. Scott seems to have been convinced that when the spirits of the dead appeared it was meant as an omen of some kind.

After the death of his wife, Scott was sure that her spirit appeared to him on several occasions. As recorded in his diary, on 12 September 1826, while he was planning a trip to London, he heard his wife's voice whispering in his ear, telling him not to go. At other times Sir Walter was sure that he felt her presence lying in the bed beside him. More disturbing to Scott was the appearance in 1826 of the spectre of Colonel Thomas Huxley, his niece's husband, at his bedside. Huxley had committed suicide and the phantom that visited Scott that night stood with blood soaking through the cravat around its neck, seemingly struggling to speak to him. Sir Walter was badly shaken by this encounter. The other world had certainly impinged itself on his reality. But as one who actively sought out the supernatural, he could hardly expect anything else.

His visit to Rosslyn Chapel, accompanied by a dowser named Annie Wilson, may have generated an amusing anecdote for Scott to repeat, but he copied the ceiling at Rosslyn on to that at Abbotsford Library. This reveals another trait of Scott's. He played down his interest in the occult, often making a joke about a subject in which he was passionately interested.

In the same way, on a tour of the Shetland Islands in August 1814, he visited Bessie Millie who he described as 'an old hag . . . upwards of ninety' who made her living by 'selling winds'. As Scott recorded, each captain about to set off paid Bessie sixpence to boil a kettle of water over which a prayer and 'magic words' were recited. She reminded Scott of Hecate, the frightful goddess of evil around whose shoulders serpents hissed. Sir Walter finished on a note of scepticism, but could not hide his evident fascination with this living practitioner of the white, or black, arts any more than he seems to have believed that he was visited by a poltergeist. On Wednesday 29 April 1818, at a time when Abbotsford was undergoing major building works, Scott was woken at 2am by a series of loud noises. The following morning he was disturbed at the same time by what he described as the sound of several men 'hard at work putting up boards and furniture'. Scott went to investigate but was unable to find any explanation to account for the noise. And was also sure that with doors and windows locked there was no way for anyone to have got in. A few days later, Scott learned that the builder responsible for the work at Abbotsford had died on that Wednesday evening between nine and ten o'clock. Sir Walter was sure that the incident that occurred was both an omen and a signal of the man's death, a communication from the other world to this.

Maybe the home he was rebuilding, Abbotsford, even then filled with weird objects, was developing a life of its own, opening its portals to the worlds beyond. Perhaps Scott was doing more than just cramming magic objects into the army of oak chests visitors encountered. It's no stretch of the imagination to believe that Scott may have dabbled with powers outside those of this earth. He had plenty of friends, the writer James Hogg for one, who shared his obsession with the supernatural.

There's only a short step from looking to practising, and Scott, a man of inquiring mind, one suspects, stuck his toe into the waters of the occult to test the reaction. That may explain why even these days it is said that strange voices and footsteps may be heard in parts of Abbotsford, Scott's very own magical creation. So the nickname applied to Scott, The Wizard of the North, may be appropriate in a way that its inventor never really intended.

4

The Occult Re-Emerges and Blossoms

By the time of the Victorian era in the nineteenth century, superstition and the supernatural were supposedly a thing of the past. But, in fact, this period witnessed the emergence of a bizarre phenomenon in the rise of Spiritualism, a belief that the dead could be contacted through certain individuals called mediums, who had the ability to communicate with the spirits of the departed. It was also a time when well-known figures, including the writer Arthur Conan Doyle, spread belief in all kinds of strange phenomena, including the existence of fairies.

Many famous individuals were in receipt of spirit messages, from the most famous general of the period, Douglas Haig, to the inventive genius that was John Logie Baird and up to and including Queen Victoria herself.

Queen Victoria

Surely it could not have been moral outrage alone that led King Edward VII to act as he did? As Prince of Wales he had earned notoriety for his womanising, self-indulgence and love

Queen Victoria and John Brown

of a good time. He was hardly a shining example of upright behaviour. And with his mother, Queen Victoria, in her grave did anyone now care what the true nature of her relationship had been with her long-dead servant John Brown? The scandal, if it was one, surely died with her. No. There was something more, a secret which caused nervous ripples and unease among royal circles. Sexual scandal they could stomach, there had been plenty of those over the years, but a queen involved in psychic contact and magic? That was something that really needed burying. And the sooner the better.

So shortly after his mother's death on 22 January 1901 at Osborne House on the Isle of Wight, Edward VII ordered the destruction or removal of any busts or memorabilia connected to John Brown. On a hill overlooking Balmoral, the cairn Victoria had erected to Brown's memory was knocked down till nothing remained except a wide circle of stones. And still it went on. A life-sized portrait of Brown, dressed in tweeds and a kilt, commissioned in 1883 after his death and hanging in Windsor Castle was taken down and given, free of charge, to William Brown, John's brother, all details of its existence being deleted from royal records.

As can be guessed by his actions, Edward, as the Prince of Wales, had long resented John Brown's influence on his mother, the Queen. Brown had even been known to stop the prince calling on Victoria if he felt she was too tired to receive visitors, no matter how exalted. Other leading figures of the day too, who felt that a mere servant had got above himself, were angered by the off-handed way Brown spoke to them and the barrier he placed between them and the Queen.

So there were plenty of influential figures who had reason to wish his memory buried and the man forgotten, and with Victoria gone, who was there to stop them? But was there more to it than simple irritation that a servant, in that class-conscious era, had given himself unwanted airs? In truth, rumours that the Queen had treated Brown as far more than a mere Highland help had circulated for years. In fact, it had grown legs and actually reached the printed page. In a pamphlet written by Alexander Robertson and published in the 1880s, the author went as far as to assert that Brown had married the Queen at a secret ceremony in Switzerland in 1868, seven years after the death of Prince Albert. He claimed that members of the royal family had attended, and even acted as witnesses. Robertson also wrote that Brown regularly visited the Queen's bedroom at night when they thought no one would catch them alone together.

The whole story might have appeared as no more than the gossip which, by the nature of things, attaches itself to public figures, except that Robertson claimed he had a witness to sexual activity between Queen Victoria and her supposed servant. He stated in his pamphlet that John Macgregor, who had been the chief wood manager on the Atholl estate, had told him that Brown and Victoria had taken a trip to Loch Ordie and along the way had been observed engaging in sexual intercourse. Whether as a result of this or another encounter, nine months later in Switzerland, a child was born. Robertson suggested it had been the arrival of the newborn infant that had led to the marriage between the pair. He also claimed that the relationship between the Queen and Brown and the birth of a child were well known around Europe. It's worth noting that Robertson was never prosecuted for libel, though if he was simply lying he had obviously broken the law. His claims were noted by the Court, but no action was taken to challenge his assertions.

But was there any substance to his claims? At the time that Robertson asserted that John Brown and Victoria had married and that the Queen had borne Brown's son, Victoria would have been forty-nine years old, which would have ranked as a very late birth for a woman of that age in the nineteenth century, though admittedly not impossible. However, Robertson's claim has been understandably ridiculed and dismissed, apart from the sheer unlikelihood of the event, on the grounds that the Queen herself had passed childbearing age, her last offspring, Beatrice, having been born in 1857 several years before her alleged pregnancy to Brown. Moreover, it has been argued, Victoria suffered from a prolapse of the womb which would have made her unable to fall pregnant or bear a child. However, it is clear that Robertson was simply repeating and attempting to provide proof for rumours regarding the birth of a child that had been circulating for years. Furthermore, the issue of Victoria's inability to have children was only confirmed at the post mortem examination following her death and might not have applied at the time Robertson was referring to.

However, it has to be agreed that the suggestion that these events took place stretches credulity, but that does not mean that strange things were not happening. So what could have been behind all these rumours? Was it a case of no smoke without a fire? To cast some light on it all, we need to step back a few years to a bizarre event involving Angus Mackay, who had been appointed Royal Piper in 1843. By the early 1850s he was making strange claims, whispering to people that he and the Queen were married. But what kind of 'marriage' did he have in mind? There were soon moves to get Mackay out of the way, but rather than simply dismiss him, Albert had him committed to Bethlehem Royal Hospital in Lambeth, London, in 1854. He was placed in the care of Dr Charles Hood, and after a few months of treatment he was released, though it's unclear as to whether Mackay was seen as 'cured' or 'incurable'. Soon after in 1855, Angus Mackay was found drowned in the River Nith in Dumfriesshire. Suicide was assumed, though if one is looking for a more sinister motive, his death was convenient for the royals if there was something that the powers above did not want to be revealed, such as Albert and Victoria's fascination for strange rituals, one aspect of which can be symbolic rather than true marriage.

Mackay has been forgotten, whereas the memory of John Brown and his close association with Victoria lives on and refuses to die away. So who was this John Brown whose name was to become so closely linked with the Queen? He was born in Crathie parish on 8 December 1826, the second son and namesake of John Brown, a tenant farmer. The future servant of Queen Victoria finished his formal education at the age of fourteen and then, as was the custom at the time, worked at a variety of menial jobs in the local area. The Balmoral estate already existed, although it was not owned by the royal family until 1852, and John Brown was taken on as a ghillie sometime in the 1840s. It was a move that transformed his life, to such an extent that by the time of his death in March 1883 the Queen wrote to John Brown's sisters-in-law in the most intimate terms. 'Weep with me', the letter went, 'for we all have lost the truest heart that ever beat! As for me my grief is dreadful. I know not how to bear it. We parted all so well and happy at dear Balmoral. And dear, dear John! My dearest, best friend, to whom I could say everything and who watched over and protected me so kindly. You have your husbands, but I have no strong arm to lean on now.' When Victoria expressed herself in this way about a servant, is it any wonder rumours circulated over the true nature of their relationship? But how had the two, miles apart in social class and background, become so intimate? Chance certainly played its part.

By the late 1840s Prince Albert made it known that he was looking for a place in Scotland to set up a home. But why

Deeside, and why Balmoral? At this time there was no local railway, and located in the middle of the country, it was a trek to get there even from the nearest large city, Aberdeen. London and Buckingham Palace would have seemed a long way away. It is claimed that Albert liked the area because it reminded him of the countryside where he had grown up in Germany. It has also been suggested Sir James Clark, the Queen's physician, told the royals that the area around Braemar would have a positive effect on the Queen's health, in particular being good for her rheumatism. Albert had a report prepared covering the geography of Balmoral and the climate. He was told, it is said, that it was 'one of the driest areas in the country'. If that is correct, he was badly informed, as Balmoral though not as wet as places along the west coast of the Highlands, is most certainly not amongst the driest parts of Scotland. In addition, it should be remembered that Balmoral has recorded some of the lowest winter temperatures in Scotland at minus twenty-seven degrees centigrade. In summer the temperature rarely gets above seventeen degrees centigrade. I readily admit that Braemar is one of my favourite spots, but it's debatable that you would spend a long time there, especially out of the summer months, for the intention of improving your health.

No, Prince Albert and Queen Victoria were set upon a place in this area for a different reason and one that says a lot about their shared interest in the other world. One fact that has been overlooked in previous discussions of Albert and Victoria's obsession with Balmoral is its particular location. The estate sits at the end of Glenshee, the Glen of the Fairies. 'Shee' comes from the Gaelic word *sithean*, which means a hill associated with supernatural beings, a part of the landscape where this world, the one we live in, interacts with the mystical worlds beyond. The area in which Balmoral is situated is interlaced with mystic locations, sites where those with an interest in psychic contact could more easily communicate with entities not of this world.

But if so, was John Brown the medium, used first by Prince Albert and then, following his death, by Queen Victoria? Critics have tried to deny that Victoria participated in spirit contact. However, during her lifetime there was intense interest in attempts to call up the dead. Leading figures of the day, including royalty, regularly took part in séances. Napoleon III and the Empress Eugenie of France made no secret of their involvement with the leading medium of the day, Daniel Home, as did Queen Sophia of Holland and the Tsar of Russia. Victoria was in regular contact with her fellow monarchs and was well aware of the current passion for Spiritualism. In fact, it was claimed regularly in spiritualist publications that Victoria was herself a practising spiritualist and had invited well-known mediums of the day to her various residences. There is, however, no clear evidence to support this, and that is because her interest in the world beyond was so strange and personal that she would never have allowed a well-known figure like Daniel Home to take part in her psychic activities. It was all a private affair and one she intended to keep to herself. Contact with the dead can be a very personal matter, and beyond those directly involved, does anyone else need to know?

Prince Albert trusted John Brown completely to look after Victoria and was quite content to disappear into the woods around Balmoral and stay at the house he had built on a remote part of the estate so that he could enjoy days away alone. Naturally, it led to speculation as to just what he was up to. Taking part in some strange rituals was one suggestion, though again the direct evidence is lacking, as is early confirmation of John Brown's mediumistic abilities. Queen Victoria did make an oblique reference to these before Prince

Albert's death, however. In March 1861 Victoria's mother, the Duchess of Kent, died. Victoria remembered that as they had left Balmoral with no inkling that her mother would soon be in her grave, John Brown had been reluctant to see them go. He had talked of illness and expressed the hope that there would be no deaths in the family. He said that he wanted to see them all return safely to Balmoral. Victoria saw it as a prophecy and a warning and appeared impressed by Brown's foresight.

There were no rumours at this point, however, that Brown and Victoria were other than Queen and servant. But did the death of her husband on 14 December 1861 throw Victoria into the world of spirits and John Brown's arms? Or did she just build on earlier involvement? And what part did Brown, in reality, play in this part of her life?

The death of Albert was a strange event in itself. Clearly aware that he was suffering from typhoid though claiming there was nothing wrong with him, his doctors, Sir James Clark and Dr William Jenner, made no effort to treat him. They even assured Victoria that there was no reason to be alarmed. Albert went down rapidly, dying in the Blue Room at Windsor Castle. The manner of his death has puzzled royal watchers ever since. Why was he simply left to die? And then why did Victoria avoid attending the funeral? She claimed that she was overwhelmed by grief, but she was by this time a mature adult with huge experience of public life and of behaving properly in the public eye. It has been speculated that there was more to it than simply emotional disturbance. And the evidence is in the actions she took to preserve Albert's memory. It seems clear that Victoria simply did not believe that Albert was dead. He had simply changed to a different form of existence, one that she could continue to have a relationship with.

Many widows, no doubt, are anxious to preserve the memory

of a loved husband, but Victoria by anyone's standards went to extreme lengths. As a first step she had every single item that had been present at the time of Albert's death in the Blue Room photographed in its place, with clear instructions to staff that nothing must ever be moved. Everything would remain as it was on the night that the Prince died. Next a photographer captured the Prince as he lay in death on his mattress. Forever after Victoria hung this ghoulish souvenir above her bed. A plaster cast was then taken of Albert's right hand. She kept this memento on her bedside table and would stroke it gently before going to bed where she would, while attempting to go to sleep, press the dead Albert's nightclothes to her chest.

After Albert's death rumours intensified over John Brown's relationship with the Queen. The actions she took, as in having a bust of Brown sculptured in 1869 for herself, didn't help matters. William Blunt, a diarist of the time who mixed in royal circles, recorded:

Brown was a rude unmannerly fellow, but had unbounded influence with the Queen whom he treated with little respect. It was the talk of all the household that he was the Queen's stallion. [It was said] that the Queen, who had been passionately in love with her husband, got it into her head that somehow the Prince's spirit had passed into Brown, and four years after her widowhood, being very unhappy, allowed him all privileges. She used to go away with him to a little house in the hills where, on the pretence that it was for protection and 'to look after the dogs', he had a bedroom next to hers.

The accuracy of this claim by Blunt has been challenged. However, it undoubtedly captures the spirit of speculation at the time, and the widespread knowledge of a close relationship between Brown and Victoria that had become far too obvious to escape attention.

Victoria may well have found Brown attractive physically, but there was clearly more to it than that. Albert had introduced Victoria to the aura of the other worlds and it was this, I would suggest, that led her into an intense relationship with a supposed servant. Victoria would hardly have risked her position of queen and the memory of Albert to whom there can be no doubt she was devoted if there had not been a bigger picture. And that bigger picture was more than straightforward contact with the spirit of the dead Albert. It was the reappearance of his form either through the medium of John Brown or as a phantom in its own right. It's well known among psychics that the spirits of the deceased are attached to familiar things. Hence ghosts haunt the spots where they lived while on earth. So Victoria kept Albert's room at Windsor as it was at the moment he died. Albert also loved Balmoral. So what better place to keep in touch with the spirit form of the man she loved than here?

Victoria, no matter the well-known photographs of a stern, resolute monarch, had more than one side to her. She published a diary of her life in the Highlands, a unique event for a monarch, and wanted to do the same with a more detailed account of the later period of her life at Balmoral, apparently containing many references to John Brown. Royal officials banned it and it has never seen the light of day, supposedly destroyed after her death, along with other sensitive material. The Queen also, by all accounts, enthusiastically took part in Halloween celebrations at Balmoral, orchestrated by John Brown. At the 1866 event a huge bonfire was built in front of the castle and, following a procession, an effigy known as Shandy Dann, a female witch, had accusations of evil practices read out to her before being consigned to the flames.

There was a streak to the Queen that does come across as odd. In her diary entry of 11 October 1852, she records:

Albert had already killed a stag, and on the road he lay. I sat down and scratched a little sketch of him [the stag] on a bit of paper that Macdonald had in his pocket. [Her husband meanwhile shot a second stag.] Albert joined us in twenty minutes, unaware of having killed the stag. What a delightful day!

Is it being over sensitive to suggest that Victoria's comment that it was 'a delightful day' strikes the ear as downright strange, or is that reading too much into it? She was certainly a woman of many parts, so different to the image that has come down to us.

The Queen's preoccupation with John Brown and her dead husband played a profound part in British history. It, for a time, made her a figure of fun and ridicule. She withdrew for years from public life, leading to an upsurge in support for an end to the monarchy and the creation of a republic. It was only later on in life, following the death of Brown, the man through whom she could contact the dead, that she re-emerged from the shadows. Reputedly, when he lay dying, the former Prime Minister Benjamin Disraeli was asked if Queen Victoria should be sent for. He replied, 'Please no, she'll only want me to take a message to Albert'.

Charles Piazzi Smyth

Sometimes an interest in the occult can bring unforeseen consequences even when one is trying to enlighten the world. For centuries the Great Pyramid of Khufu standing on the

Giza plateau near the city of Cairo in Egypt has aroused awe in all those who have visited it. For thousands of years it was the tallest man-made structure on the planet, supreme till the Eiffel Tower outstripped it in height in 1889. But is it anything other than a magnificent monument, a testimony to man's ingenuity and creative ability? One individual, Charles Piazzi Smyth, for over forty years the Astronomer Royal of Scotland, was convinced that there was far more to it than just that.

For an outwardly Christian man and a scientist, the belief that the Great Pyramid at Khufu contained mystical symbolism and hidden messages for mankind might appear at odds with each other. But then Charles Piazzi Smyth was not straightforward by any means. His appointment to the post of Astronomer Royal in 1846 at the comparatively tender age of twenty-seven, a position he then held till 1888, might have caused a bit of a stir, but Piazzi Smyth was fortunate in having influential friends. His father was president of the British Royal Astronomical Society, whilst his application was supported by the world famous astronomer, Sir John Herschel. To be fair, encouraged by his father, Piazzi Smyth had followed a lifelong interest in the heavens. He had spent several years at an observatory in South Africa studying the stars and planets and could have been seen as having the potential to develop astronomy in Scotland and raise its stature in the world. And it can hardly be denied that Piazzi Smyth in his lifetime achieved that aim. He is remembered, among other contributions to astronomy, for his pioneering work in placing telescopes at high altitudes to obtain a clearer view of the heavens.

However, in his forties he developed a taste for more occult research. Or did it simply become more obvious? In fact, on the face of it Piazzi Smyth did a complete about-turn. One minute he was denying in his writings and lectures that the Great Pyramid at Giza was anything more than a magnificent monument, a burial place for pharaoh Khufu. The next he had abandoned his duties at the observatory and in November 1864 sailed to Egypt having, like a St Paul on the road to Damascus, become suddenly convinced that he had a mission to discover the mysteries hidden within the pyramids. What was even odder was that he appeared to be suggesting that his venture was divinely inspired, as if he had received a message from another world and had been given a new role in life. Colleagues who had always regarded him as a safe pair of hands were simply stunned.

However, was there more going on beneath the surface than was obvious at first glance? Piazzi Smyth's appointment as Scotland's head astronomer may appear a little less straightforward when we consider some other factors. He was a close associate of the Clerk family of Penicuik, who themselves were involved in some odd practices. It's true that the Clerk family had played a leading role in the scientific and cultural milieu of Scotland. Sir James Clerk Maxwell, the world-famous scientist recognised for his work in electro-magnetism and electrodynamics, was a cousin of the main branch of the family. The Clerk family name had been established by Sir John Clerk, a lawyer, antiquary and musician, as far back as the seventeenth century. His contribution to cultural development is recognised by an entry in the *Encyclopaedia of Scotland*. The Clerk family carried weight in Edinburgh circles, and Piazzi Smyth had become a close chum of Henry Clerk, son of Sir George Clerk, who was seen as the head of the family, as fathers were in those Victorian times.

But there was another side to the Clerk family. Sir John Clerk had been involved in some strange practices. Obsessed with the beliefs of the ancient world he had a shaft dug into the side of a hill on his estate. Inside this tunnel he built a small room carved out of solid rock, which he decorated with strange symbols and motifs. It was within this structure that with friends and followers he took part in rituals which we can only speculate on as no details have ever been forthcoming. Clerk was also friendly with James St Clair, the owner of Rosslyn Chapel, and in 1736 encouraged him to carry out repairs to the church which had been damaged some fifty years earlier. Clerk was a prominent Freemason and 1736 was also the year that the Freemasons' Grand Lodge of Scotland was founded.

So there were two facets to the Clerk family, a tradition of scientific interest, contrasted with an interest in mysticism and the wonders of the ancients. It may be that Charles Piazzi Smyth's involvement with the family through his acquaintance with Henry Clerk led to the sudden Eureka moment that drove him down a very strange path. So intense did Smyth's involvement with the pyramids become that he named one of his daughters Rosetta in honour of the famous stone tablet discovered in 1799, which, after it was deciphered, enabled Europeans to read for the first time the hieroglyphs of ancient Egypt.

So what was it about the pyramids that so intrigued Piazzi Smyth that he abandoned all his scientific training for the proverbial will-of-the wisp? Smyth had managed to convince himself that such an enormous structure as the Great Pyramid could not have been built by human effort alone. There must have been supernatural assistance of some kind. In the atmosphere of the time, Piazzi Smyth could only ascribe this to divine intervention. He came to believe that the proof was to be found in the relationship between the various dimensions of the different parts of the Great Pyramid, that the measurements embodied in its construction would provide a link to accounts given in the Bible, crucially that the tribes of

Israel and whoever erected the pyramids had used a common unit of length.

Whatever Smyth set off to achieve, the result, in practice, was to set a huge ball rolling, one which not only veered way off his intended course but has continued to the present day, inspiring a legion of claims over the origins and function of the pyramids. Were they intended as museums of secret information to be preserved for future generations? Or even set up by alien beings to allow them to communicate with their distant homeland? Thanks to Piazzi Smyth, the theories are simply never-ending.

But when Smyth put forward the suggestion that divine intervention had contributed in some way to the erection of the pyramids, did he have only the Christian god in mind? His three-volume publication on his work at Giza, detailing all the measurements he recorded, is an undoubted achievement, though a difficult read for the non-specialist – as I can testify! His commitment to his research cannot be doubted, but it was the road that it was leading him down that puzzled friends. Smyth became fixated on the idea that the building of the Great Pyramid could be slotted into the chronology of the past, as detailed in the Biblical texts. This was doubly confusing, as even by the time Smyth was conducting his investigation in the 1860s, the Bible as reliable history had largely been discredited.

To prove his theory, Smyth took up and developed the ideas of a fellow astronomer, the Canadian H. G. Haliburton, who had proposed that ancient tribes had used the star cluster the Pleiades, commonly called the Seven Sisters, as a means to regulate their annual calendar. Using the data he had gathered from his work on the pyramids, Smyth argued that they had been built when the Pleiades was at its equinox and the star Draconis was on the opposite side of the pole. This would have dated the construction of the pyramids to the exact date of 2173 BC, a calculation which he believed to his own satisfaction fitted with and supported history as laid down in the Bible.

The fact that no academic or learned society took his conclusions seriously is neither here nor there. The impact Smyth had on the popular imagination then and now has been immense. The calculations that he detailed and made available revealed all manner of strange relationships between the dimensions of different parts of the Great Pyramid. To take one instance, the height of the pyramid bore the same relationship to its perimeter, as does the radius of a circle to its circumference. So it appeared the Egyptians knew the value of pi over 3,000 years before it was believed to have been discovered. But any scientific value of Smyth's work was quickly overshadowed by the interpretations of its mystical potential. Soon people were proclaiming that by examining the measurements inside and outside, not only the past but also the future could be discovered. And what of those links to the stars that Smyth had proposed? Did they have a greater significance than merely a symbolic one? Was there also a connection to the planet Mars, popularly believed at this time to be or have been inhabited?

Unintentionally, Smyth founded the science of pyramidology, the belief that these structures of ancient Egypt offer a clue to a range of possibilities including contact with alien beings and a passageway to other dimensions. Though ignored by his fellow scientists, Smyth attracted a vast and influential following, including James Garfield, the twentieth President of the United States. Smyth opened a Pandora's box of weird ideas which, no matter how discredited, simply refuse to go away. They are as popular now as when they first emerged one hundred and fifty years ago.

Smyth's scientific research has largely been forgotten. Even the work he carried out on the pyramids has come to be seen as badly flawed by archaeologists used to more thorough measuring techniques. The data Piazzi Smyth painstakingly compiled simply wasn't accurate enough, but the cult he inadvertently founded and the people for whom Smyth is celebrated as the first person who truly realised the mystic potential of the ancient pyramids live on.

Arthur Conan Doyle

The mysteries of the East have proved an ideal setting for many fictional detectives. Legions of phantoms from Ancient Egypt have been overcome in books, movies and computer games. But for one character it was different. There can be little doubt that, in a reversal of fortune, it was the spirit world that triumphed over Sherlock Holmes. His creator, Arthur Conan Doyle, had developed an obsession with the paranormal that baffled most of his admirers. One of the enduring mysteries is how a man who seemed by nature a practical type, who studied medicine at Edinburgh University and practised as a doctor, an individual who did not retreat from but interacted with the world, standing twice for Parliament and taking up some infamous causes such as the wrongful conviction for murder of Oscar Slater, could so readily convince himself of the most unlikeliest of phenomena, including the existence of fairies.

Arthur Conan Doyle was born in a flat in Picardy Place, Edinburgh, on 22 May 1859. At the age of ten he was sent to Stonyhurst College in Lancashire, a school run by the Jesuits. After a spell in Austria to learn German he attended Edinburgh University, encouraged by his family to take up medicine as a career. It's not clear why or when Conan Doyle became so fixated with the supernatural. He wasn't always so easily persuaded that the world of phantoms existed, or so he claimed.

In 1881, as a newly qualified doctor, he secured a position as a ship's medical officer on the African Steam Navigation Company's cargo liner the *Mayumba*. On his first voyage to Nigeria he fell seriously ill, probably from malaria. He later wrote: 'I remember staggering to my bunk and then all was blotted out. As I was myself a doctor there was no one to look after me and I lay for several days fighting it out with Death. It speaks well for my constitution that I came out a victor. I remember no psychic experience, no visions, no fears, nothing save a nightmare fog.' 'Selecting a Ghost', one of his earlier short stories published in 1883, even poked fun at the occult, but within a few years, it was all to be very different.

Conan Doyle, however, may have been influenced by his father, Charles, an Irishman who was steeped in tales of nature spirits and made drawings of these entities. Conan Doyle's uncle, Richard, was well known as a painter of goblins, fairies and elves and even claimed to have seen them in real life. Conan Doyle, in later years, talked of his father's 'wild and strange fantasies' and of the water-colours he drew of 'dancing witches' and 'goblins chasing children across churchyards'. It would be surprising if the parent's fascination with the occult had not rubbed off on Conan Doyle. But, on the other hand, as his father had been consigned to a mental institution it might, it could be thought, have had the opposite effect, turning him away from the supernatural rather than pulling him into its embrace.

In spite of what Doyle later claimed, that he had been attracted to the paranormal only in later life, the evidence suggests the contrary. Was he really as sceptical of the occult in his early years as he later wrote? When he was twenty-one years old Doyle had attended a lecture in Birmingham titled 'Does Death End All', given by an American spiritualist. He was interested, but not, he wrote, convinced. Even when working as a doctor in Southsea, Doyle was still referring to the supernatural as 'nonsense' and 'unscientific'. His notes from this period, however, list nearly a hundred books on the subject of Spiritualism. Whether or not he believed, he was regularly involved in experiments with telepathy, hypnosis and contacting the spirit world through table tapping. The truth, it seems, is that he simply kept quiet at this stage about his interest in the paranormal – perhaps for professional reasons. There were hints though of what was to come.

His first published story, 'The Mystery of Sarassa Valley', was based on an African legend about a fierce-eyed supernatural demon that terrifies local villagers. It appeared in the periodical *Chambers Journal* in 1879 and so predates the arrival of Sherlock Holmes in the story 'A Study in Scarlet' by several years. In fact, looking back, it may be wondered that Holmes ever appeared at all, for by the time the detective first showed up in the *Beeton's Christmas Annual* of 1887, Conan Doyle was well down the road to spiritualist belief. He later admitted that as early as 1880 when he had been working aboard the ship the *Hope* he was already 'a believer in something I later identified as Spiritualism'. What would have shocked his fans to the core was the strange fact that Conan Doyle did not like Sherlock Holmes as a character, even though it brought him international acclaim and financial success. He killed off Holmes as soon as he decently could in 1893. The fictional detective was given an early exit, with his famous death leap at the Reichenbach Falls in the embrace of the arch criminal Professor Moriarty, because Conan Doyle was rapidly heading in another direction, a campaign to promote the cause of the supernatural.

Even as Conan Doyle wrote Sherlock Holmes' obituary he was busy on what is generally agreed to be a semi-autobiographical novel with the title *The Stark Munro Letters*. It was in sharp contrast to the Holmes stories, dealing with aspects of religion and revealing his growing obsession with Spiritualism. It's clear that Conan Doyle was anxious to get rid of the world's number one detective so that he could work on spreading the news that, though Holmes was fictional, the other world by contrast was real and all around us. *The Stark Munro Letters* failed to arouse much interest, though it generated considerable bemused comment. Why would a writer kill off his most famous creations to produce such a bizarre and largely unreadable novel? Conan Doyle was in his turn puzzled by the public's response. The reaction to the death of Sherlock Holmes mystified and even irritated him. It may seem bizarre that an author should wish to end the life of his most lucrative fictional character, but Conan Doyle had no remorse over the decision he had taken. In April 1893 he wrote to his mother that he was finishing the last story involving Sherlock Holmes and then the 'gentleman vanishes, never to reappear'. He added with obvious feeling, 'I am weary of his name'.

Conan Doyle hoped that his now almost forgotten historical novels would establish his reputation as a great writer, but he soon lost interest in writing altogether as his mind turned more and more to proving the existence of spirit entities. In 1887 he had written to the leading spiritualist newspaper of the time, *Light*, to publicly announce his belief in the reality of supernatural phenomena. However, under pressure from both the public and publishers, and perhaps tempted by the huge sums of money on offer, Doyle produced a second set of Sherlock Holmes short stories. His heart, however, was not really in it, but he saw the cash earned as a useful tool for promoting the cause of the spirit world in all its guises.

It led him down some bizarre paths. During the summer of 1917, Elsie Wright and her ten-year-old cousin Frances Griffiths from the village of Cottingly in Yorkshire played together in a narrow brook, known locally as a beck, just behind Elsie's garden in Main Street. Here the girls claimed to have encountered fairies and other spirits and, to prove it, took photographs of these entities. By June 1920 these snaps had come to the attention of Conan Doyle, who described them as 'epoch making'. Even though his friend and fellow spiritualist, the famous scientist Sir Oliver Lodge, denounced them as fakes, Conan Doyle went on the campaign trail convinced that he had found evidence that would prove the existence of other worlds. The result was Conan Doyle's most derided work, *The Coming of the Fairies*, published in 1922, in which he wrote: 'I have convinced myself that there is overwhelming evidence for the fairies'. It was another event that left fans of Sherlock Holmes puzzled.

It was to be sixty years before Elsie Wright admitted to the world that it had been a hoax, but that is not the end of the story because Frances Griffiths, on the other hand, stuck to her account that they truly had seen fairies, and that though not all the pictures were genuine, some were. Conan Doyle was long dead by this time and during his life was convinced that fairies and other denizens of the nature spirit sort existed. He even put plaster statues of gnomes in his garden to encourage the fairies to come and visit. Sherlock Holmes would surely have scratched his head in wonder. But to Doyle, Holmes was fiction; the spirit world was fact. Nothing was too weird that Conan Doyle would not believe it if he had witnessed it with his own eyes.

In 1923 during a trip to Canada, Conan Doyle attended a

séance during which water from a tap was supposedly turned into wine. Doyle was sure that he had witnessed a miracle and the event confirmed his belief that Jesus had simply been a medium with exceptional psychic powers. So convinced was Doyle of the existence of the other side that he wasn't even worried that his son, Kingsley, serving in France during World War I might be killed. In May 1917 he wrote: 'I do not fear death for Kingsley', as to a 'convinced spiritualist death became rather an uncaring thing'. To Doyle, dying was a pleasant experience, as had been confirmed by the spirit messages he had received which described the departed soul entering a spirit body with the promise of a good life to follow.

Perhaps it wasn't surprising then that after Kingsley's death from Spanish Flu in 1918, followed soon after by that of his brother Innes, Conan Doyle could claim that he felt closer to them than ever. At a séance in Wales he was convinced that Kingsley had 'come through' and kissed him on the forehead. To Conan Doyle it was all part of a great plan for which he had been destined. He claimed that God had put him in a special position to encourage the public to believe in life after death.

It all seemed so odd coming from a man who looked as stolid as a walrus and who had produced in Sherlock Holmes the detached observer *par excellence*. But just how straightforward and stable was Conan Doyle? His father had been obsessed with the supernatural and ended up in an asylum for the mentally insane. And while his father was still alive, his mother formed a strange attachment to a man almost half her age. In 1876, twenty-two-year old Bryan Waller joined Mary and Charles Doyle as a lodger at their flat at 2 Argyle Park in Edinburgh. Soon after, Mary, at thirty-nine, fell pregnant with her ninth child. Bizarrely, and in a move which has raised eyebrows ever since, the child was given Waller's Christian name even though she was a girl. The daughter, christened Bryan Mary, was born on 2 March 1877. Some have doubted that a young man such as Bryan Waller would have been attracted to an older woman, as Mary was when they met. Life, however, tells a different story. And the relationship, whatever its nature, continued for many years.

When Waller graduated with a degree in medicine he bought a large house and Charles and Mary Doyle moved in with him. He certainly seems to have had a hand in having Conan Doyle's father committed to the institution from which he was never to emerge. And when Waller inherited his father's estate in Yorkshire in 1883, Mary abandoned Edinburgh and with her three younger children moved into a house in the grounds, where she lived rent-free for more than thirty years. She refused all efforts by Conan Doyle to have her come and live with him. Even after Waller's marriage in 1896, Mary stayed on the estate, often visited by Waller to the irritation, it is said, of his new wife. It was not till 1917 that Mary left Waller and moved in with her world-famous son. Conan Doyle never seems to have objected to Waller's presence in his mother's life. It was Waller, in fact, who suggested to Doyle that he take up medicine and coached him through the entrance exams.

But, of course, Conan Doyle had his own skeletons in the closet. In 1885 he had married Louise Hawkins, known as Touie, who within a few years was to be diagnosed with tuberculosis. She fought the disease over a considerable period, surviving till 1906, though apparently an invalid for much of the time. Long before she finally succumbed, however, Conan Doyle had met and fallen in love with Jean Leckie who he married within a year of his wife's death. There is no doubt that Conan Doyle was under strain during this period and it has been speculated that his passion for the afterlife was a response to the emotional problems that confronted him in his personal life.

In fact, the other world, as it turned out, had Conan Doyle very much in their thoughts. The spirit called Pheneas was of particular comfort to him, and, as it transpired, his new wife Jean Leckie possessed the psychic ability to communicate with the departed. Pheneas made his first contact through Jean in December 1922. According to the messages she received, Pheneas had been a scribe in the Babylonian city of Ur around 3,000 BC. This ancient phantom quickly became Conan Doyle's must trusted and familiar spirit. Doyle even asked Pheneas for personal advice, consulting him over whether or not he should visit the USA and if he should take his children with him. When the family moved to a new home, Pheneas asked for and was given his own séance room painted in mauve, as he had requested. But with Conan Doyle nothing could be straightforward and over time Pheneas's messages became increasingly strange. Convinced of the reality of the spirit world and in particular of Pheneas, Conan Doyle published *Pheneas Speaks* in 1927, a collection of the spirit messages he had received over the years through Pheneas which included a prophecy that the world would soon be destroyed. The reaction was predictable. Conan Doyle, however, could not understand the public's unwillingness to listen to what the other side was telling them. He refused to give up his, as he saw it, great campaign to enlighten the world. He even convinced himself that Harry Houdini, the master escapologist and illusionist, used psychic power to perform his tricks. Houdini thought Conan Doyle, who he admired greatly, was simply deluding himself.

So was the brilliant writer, the creator of the iconic figure of Sherlock Holmes, a victim of his own imagination? Was he prepared to believe anything and everything people told him if it allegedly originated from the other side? Was it sensible to argue that Abraham Lincoln, the US President, had been an ardent spiritualist who had received advice from phantoms of the dead? Conan Doyle certainly did not see himself as a dupe. He had attended many séances over a lifetime, listening to and recording countless spirit messages. He was well aware that there were false mediums and that many things that took place in the séance room were the result of trickery. He simply did not believe that it was right to expose this publicly, as mediums were often under pressure to perform and so on occasion took the easy way out. His view was that such deviations were irrelevant as the overall message was undoubtedly real and true. He can be laughed at for the Cottingly fairy episode, but as one of those involved went to her grave persisting in her story that she really had seen nature spirits, maybe Conan Doyle had the last laugh in this case.

In some ways he was ahead of his time. One of his later collections of short stories, *The Maracot Deep*, published in 1929, includes the curiously titled 'When the World Screamed'. In it Conan Doyle's fictional creation Professor George Challenger, being convinced that the earth is a living organism, drills a huge channel to the earth's core and discovers a breathing, shining mass at the heart of the planet. One of his companions plunges a harpoon into the moving substance and the planet lets out an ear-shattering scream.

The concept of the earth as a living being was years ahead of its time and had to wait till the 1960s to become part of a wider belief among the New Age generation. Did Conan Doyle come to this idea through Pheneas or his other spirit messengers? He was well aware that psychic power could be used for evil but believed that on the other side a world of happiness awaited everyone. Sherlock Holmes no doubt would have looked at him good and hard and questioned the evidence. Perhaps it was because Conan Doyle could not face up to Holmes' clinical skills that he killed off the forensic, rational side of his character. And so it surely has to be agreed that it was the spirit world which won the battle for Conan Doyle's mind and, in the end, convinced him that Sherlock Holmes simply had to go.

John Logie Baird

However, was Conan Doyle right to believe that the other world can be intimate with our own? Did John Logie Baird, the father of television, get inspiration for his inventions from beyond the grave? From the invisible realm of phantoms and spirits? Baird had experienced many strange incidents from the time of his childhood. He recalled several of these in his autobiography *Television and Me*, the original version of which curiously did not appear till 1988, forty-two years after his death in 1946.

One episode that he described in detail had a particularly dramatic effect. It occurred one day when Baird, a young boy at the time, had been left by himself at home, a single-storey stone built house bought by his father the Reverend John Baird in 1881. The rest of the family had gone together to church. Bored, as in those Victorian times very little happened in Helensburgh, a small town on the Firth of Clyde, on a Sunday, John was standing by the window of his bedroom, looking out. He was aware that a strange stillness hung over the house. As he was idly eyeing up objects in the garden, an old man clutching a walking stick and bent with age appeared from the side of the house, stopped in front of John and stared up at him. Years later, Baird could recall the shock that this 'vision' had on him. He leapt back from the glass in fright, sensing even at that young age that he had glimpsed something not of this world. In fact, Logie Baird got it into his head that what he had seen was an image of himself as an old man. In his autobiography, recalling the incident, he wondered if one day he would walk up to that same window and see himself standing there as a young boy. Clearly Baird regarded this as a significant event. Had he really glimpsed himself in the future? Baird doesn't say whether in later life he encountered himself as a child, but its inclusion in his short autobiography, less than 40,000 words long, with other supernatural incidents, suggests that he took a deep interest in the impact the paranormal could have on one's life.

Surprising perhaps for a man so obsessed with technology and its potential, from an early age Baird was convinced that the spirits were all around him and very real. In later life, as a world-famous man with, it might be thought, many other events in his life to recount, he recalled that even as a child he was aware of the presence of spirits and phantoms. He described how at night he would be visited by a female spectre, dressed all in grey, and two old men who made their appearance crouching at the far end of his bed as if waiting to get hold of him. He also experienced visions of other more frightening creatures, though what form they took Baird does not tell us. If these were mere childhood fears of being left alone in a bedroom at night, why did Baird include them in such a short précis of his life? It seems clear that, in his mind at least, they represented something strange and unfathomable. But did these glimpses of other worlds encourage him to seek a way of contacting these spirits? Of actually seeing into the world they inhabited?

John Logie Baird lived a strange and mysterious life, many details of which his biographers even today have difficulty unravelling. The main outlines are not in dispute. He was born in 1888 in the seashore town of Helensburgh, educated at Glasgow Academy, followed by a period at the city's Royal Technical College, the institution that eventually became Strathclyde University. Up to this time, however, no one could have realised that Baird was a genius in the making. His academic achievements were no more than average. Following graduation he took off to Jamaica before returning to the UK where he became involved in several business ventures, including the manufacture of soap and marketing a new type of sock he had patented. Behind the scenes, however, he was secretly working on several pioneering inventions. These hit the world in 1926 when Baird, using the process he had discovered, famously transmitted a moving picture from one room to another. This was the first time this had ever been achieved. It was an epoch-making event. In 1927 he did the same from London to Glasgow and in 1928 succeeded in a transmission across the Atlantic. So far so good. But events apparently went downhill after these fantastic early successes, achievements which have made his name for all time. Infamously, the BBC experimenting with the new medium decided against taking up Baird's process of television transmission, preferring a different method, and Baird failed to recoup the money and the effort he had invested in the creation of this device which has become so much a part of everyday life. After this failure, Baird faded into comparative obscurity.

Recent research by his admirers, however, suggests a quite different version, that far from turning into the forgotten man of legend, Baird was taken up by the government and was involved in many secret projects, projects so secret that even today the authorities refuse to acknowledge the part Baird played in them. Fibre optics and radar are only two developments it's said Baird made a huge but hidden contribution to. There are many more, including colour television and the video recorder.

But what evidence are these claims based on? The obvious one relates to the outbreak of World War II. At a time when anyone with ideas on the development of new technology was being signed up by the government, is it sensible to believe that a genius of the stature of Baird would be left out? That, however, is the official version. John Logie Baird, the inventor of television, was, so the story goes, quite literally left to his own devices. It's hard to believe, especially as we now know that the military were particularly interested in the potential use of TV transmission in combat situations.

Baird's own diaries for the war years give brief references to regular meetings with leading people from the world of science and from the military, including Sir Robert Watson-Watt, involved with the invention of radar, and the physicist Sir Edward Appleton. It's been suggested that it was only thanks to Baird that radar was developed, though Watson-Watt seems never to have acknowledged his major contribution. It's curious to note, in this context, that in 1944 Baird wrote in his diary that he had taken out 'secret radar patents'. Exactly what this involved is unknown. It appears that Baird's name is missing from the biographies of nearly all of those well-known individuals with whom he interacted. It's all part of a very curious pattern. An obituary of Baird, printed in the *Daily Herald* on 15 June 1946 ran: 'the full story of Baird cannot yet be told. During the war he was working in his house in Sydenham [a London suburb], *not only on an invention for the government, which is still on the secret list,* but also on research of his own' [my italics]. To add to the mystery, as early as 1928 Baird was seen dressed in the uniform of a reserve army lieutenant when he was supposed to have been simply a private individual working on the development of television. The rank he sported was, it is claimed, one normally given to civilians enrolled on government 'special projects' of that era. Was there a reason why the authorities were determined to distance themselves publicly from John Logie Baird? Did it have something to do with his involvement with the supernatural?

In fact, Baird's encounters with the world of phantoms were by no means confined to his time as a child in Helensburgh. Paranormal incidents in the 1920s, even as he focussed on the creation of television, impacted on his consciousness and made an appearance in his autobiography. One such event happened while he was lodging at a house in the London borough of Ealing. Baird was lying in bed at night when the door handle was turned slowly and quietly till the door stood slightly open. He was aware of a presence that didn't enter but instead silently moved away. The event was repeated every night for the time that Baird lived there. If it strikes one as a curious incident, even odder is Baird's explanation for it. He claims that he discovered later, though he doesn't tell us how, that the landlady's child who had the room next to Baird was afraid of the dark and, for companionship, opened Baird's door. Somewhat cruelly, one might think, Baird described the lad's act as a 'pathetic little ceremony'. One might reasonably ask that if Baird, this inventor of genius, did truly consider the incident as no more than a 'pathetic little ceremony', why he went to the trouble of including it in his exceptionally short autobiography. It only makes sense if Baird saw in it a continuation of his own experiences from his time as a child with the phantoms of the night.

During this period as Baird developed Noctovision, as 'television' was then called, he was also attending spiritualist séances. At these, dead inventors passed messages to him with advice and promised to assist him in his work. He described one of these encounters in detail. It followed the well-established pattern of these events. A circle of chairs surrounded a small sitting box, coloured black, for the medium, a woman in her thirties. Each participant held the hand of the person next to them so that the possibility of 'cheating' was reduced. Holding hands would also form a bond between the sitters which would, according to spiritualist theory, facilitate the arrivals of the spirits of the deceased. Lights were turned off, followed by singing and a prayer. As Baird watched, a shimmering cloud of purple formed. And then Baird received a message, tapped out in Morse code. It came from the inventor Thomas Edison who told Baird that he was aware of his work on Noctovision and had been experimenting with it himself in the world beyond. He warned Baird of the dangers of the invention, suggesting that this was not the right time to unleash it on the world. Baird, as we know, ignored him, but in view of the military use to which the whole concept was to be put to, one can have some sympathy with Edison.

Of course, it might be suggested that Baird included this incident merely to dismiss it. Certainly a hint of scepticism seems to hang over his account. However, that would be far from the truth. In fact, Baird quite explicitly stated that he couldn't dismiss it, as he had attended other séances that had convinced him that a genuine phenomenon was present. He explicitly made the point that new discoveries could be made through spirit contact. Had that included television? Was his reference to Edison an oblique admission that in developing this invention he had been given information from the astral plane? If Baird had lived longer we might have learned more.

However, some have turned this idea on its head and suggested that Baird was determined on developing Noctovision so that the device could be used to contact, and learn about, the world of spirits. Baird reportedly said as much though it's disputed that it formed his prime motivation. But the man who loved mechanical objects also trained himself in yoga and would sit alone in his bedroom apparently in a deep trance. He was much more than simply a man 'of the flesh'. In discussing Marconi, the inventor of the wireless, Baird made the point that the idea for the invention had come to Marconi while he was kneeling in prayer. Perhaps that was a hint from Baird that the world beyond was no phantom of the mind and could genuinely provide even the inventors of technology with inspiration.

Baird, understandably, would never have admitted that the spirits of dead geniuses influenced him. He knew that he would lose all credibility. But perhaps his interest was better known in private circles and it was this that led the authorities to distance themselves from Baird. Taking advice from the spirit world was not something that a government, if it valued its image, could ever own up to.

Douglas Haig

And that same perception of valuing one's image applied so much more when a soldier was involved. Field Marshal Douglas Haig was a man of mystery. Even close friends, of whom there were few, viewed him as an enigma. His rise to the heights as Commander-in-Chief of British forces in France during World War I puzzled many. As a child he was viewed as a bit of a dunce and failed to shine either at school or university. He only made it into Oxford thanks in the main to his family's wealth and position. As a soldier he was regarded as no more than competent, but somehow he numbered among his supporters Queen Victoria and her successor King Edward VII. He was even a welcome guest at the sovereign's private residence at Balmoral, a rare honour. And when George V eventually succeeded Edward, Haig remained a court favourite with whom the King would engage in confidential correspondence on the abilities of Haig's fellow generals. So why was Haig so favourably regarded by the top drawer of British society?

Contacts through secret societies may have played a part. Douglas's father, John Haig, owner of the world-famous whisky distillery of the same name, was a committed and enthusiastic Freemason. Douglas also enrolled in this organisation, which was more select and secretive at the time than it is today. It has been suggested that his membership was only passive, but it is noticeable that many of his friends in later years, people of influence, were also members.

Douglas Haig was born on 19 June 1861 at 24 Charlotte Square, Edinburgh. A plaque marks the location of his birthplace. In keeping with the traditions of the time, his family, on the surface, were committed Presbyterians and churchgoers. Bizarrely, however, his family were also avid spiritualists. Haig's sister Henrietta spent a lifetime engaging in automatic writing in attempts to contact the dead. Haig's mother, Rachel, was equally convinced that it was possible to converse with the spirits. She and Douglas's sisters frequently tried to communicate with the phantoms of the afterlife. Right up to her death in 1879, Rachel participated in séances. One of her last letters to Douglas, when he was seventeen, described the psychic efforts of his sister Janet, then aged thirty-two: 'Jenty is waiting for the spirits to write, but they won't answer today even though it is the anniversary of my father's death. I thought perhaps we might be able to contact him, but it is of no use'.

Oddly, the supernatural played a part in the foundation of the Haig line as far back as the thirteenth century. No less a person than the famous mystic Thomas the Rhymer, by tradition, witnessed the charter granting Petrus de Haga, from whom the Haig family descended, a castle and estate in Bemersyde, some fifty miles from Edinburgh. The Rhymer allegedly made a prediction about the family and their new estate: 'Tide what may what e'r betide, Haig shall be Haig of Bemersyde'. In other words, whatever happened the family would remain owners of Bemersyde. In later life, Douglas Haig set out to make this prophecy come true, buying back in 1923 the estate, which had by then passed out of the family's possession.

Some have suggested that Haig's interest in the spirits of the other world was no more than a sop to his favourite sister, Henrietta. But comments he made and his actions suggest an interest that was more than just a passing fad. Posted to India, Haig made a stop at Port Said, Egypt, en route. Here he consulted an Indian fortune-teller. Dorothy, his wife, also known as Doris, later claimed, in her biography of her husband *The Man I Knew*, that:

Indian fortune-tellers are generally known to be above the average. We found a wonderful man at Port Said who foretold Douglas's future like reading a map. The Great War was described and the anxieties and responsibilities entailed. Douglas was to be successful in everything that he undertook, and would save his country. Honours would be showered on him, but he would be much concerned about the sufferings around him. At the time I did not realise properly the future that this man was unfolding.

It's doubtful if Haig saw anything out of the ordinary in consulting a medium. It was a continuation of the Haig family interest in the other world, and this incident in Egypt was a part of a pattern that can be seen throughout Haig's career.

After serving for a time in India, Haig was promoted to Major General and returned to duties in the UK. Residing in London and with a heavy workload, he still found the time to visit the many psychics offering their services in the capital during this era. It appears that usually he went in the company of his sister Henrietta and wife Dorothy, though the evidence suggests that he required neither to engage in contact with the spirit world.

On 20 September 1906 Haig attended a séance with Dorothy and Henrietta at 6 Bloomfield Road, Maida Vale. The medium, Miss McCreadie, went into a trance and 'brought through' from the other side a little girl called Sunshine. Haig recorded in his diary that Sunshine:

> . . . said that I was influenced by several spirits – notably a small man named Napoleon aided me. That it was in my power to be helped by him for good affairs, but I must think of him and try and get his aid as he was always near me. Mother threw a light round me and placed on my breast a star which illuminated all about me. Hugo also sent a message. So did George.

Haig recorded in his diary another séance he attended at Peckham Rue, London, on 24 November 1908. Haig did not think much of the medium, Mr Husk, who acted as the channel to the spirit world on this occasion. He commented of the session that 'the whole is a great fraud'. However, this should not be taken as a blanket condemnation of spirit contact but a reasoned judgement that some psychics make unjustifiable claims. This downside of Spiritualism was commonly noted by even the most avid believers in the phenomenon. Whatever Haig's experience at Peckham it did not put him off receiving messages from the spirit world, as events during World War I would show.

But to what extent did his interest in the supernatural affect his career in the army and, at grassroots level, his attitude towards war? One fact is clear: Haig was no military genius and many professional soldiers thought that he had been promoted way above his ability. He took over command of the Aldershot garrison, viewed as the most important in the UK, in March 1912. During his time there he wrote several reports which have been seen as evidence of Haig's determination to modernise the British army but also as examples of his lack of understanding of the way that wars would now be fought, particularly following the decisive and unexpected defeat of Russia by Japan in the 1904–1905 conflict. Haig, to take one instance, in spite of overwhelming evidence to the contrary, insisted that there would be a continuing role for mounted cavalry in modern warfare. Nothing seemed to shake him from this conviction. As late as 17 June 1916 he wrote in his diary, 'to shorten the war and reap the fruits of any success we must make use of the mobility of the cavalry.' He was not, however, totally without insight. He wanted to move away from an officer elite made up largely of men recruited from English public and Scottish private schools. His aim was to bring in a far larger contingent of university graduates, men who he believed had been taught to think. The universities at this time were still in the main private school monopolies, so in terms of a class-based officer, the make-up would not necessarily have been significantly altered, but it did suggest that Haig was pushing for a more professional set-up where ability rather than who you knew would play a bigger role. This was in spite of the fact that he himself had largely been a beneficiary of the class system.

However, few would have predicted that this career officer who appeared no more than competent would rise to the rarefied heights of Commander of the British forces in France, responsible for the lives of millions of men and the safety of Britain. If the Great War (1914–18) was the graveyard and slaughterhouse of legend, for some it provided the opportunity to achieve a recognition that might otherwise have been barred to them. But luck, contacts and the spirit world was on-side for Douglas Haig.

Haig's confidence throughout the war that Germany was on the edge of giving up the fight was a noted aspect of his strategy. It sustained him throughout a series of defeats and the disaster of the Somme in 1916, for which he must take a share of the blame. His optimism was a mystery to many. Some saw it as a curse, as it led him to believe that one more push would bring about the collapse of German morale. So, should we seek a mystical source to explain Haig's determination and confidence?

On 4 August 1914, with the British army preparing for war, Henrietta, Haig's sister, wrote to him with a message from the world beyond the veil. It had been 'sent' by George, their dead brother, and read: 'Tell Douglas to go forward without fear because God will watch over and guide him. And he will return covered in Glory. Douglas must not forget to ask for the blessing of God on his great campaign because nothing happens by accident and God blesses those who ask Him for it'. The evidence suggests that Haig was convinced that he was, indeed, the beneficiary of supernatural help.

In July 1916, as the Somme battle was about to break, he wrote to his wife, claiming that his plan not only for the forthcoming attack but for the whole campaign had been made with divine assistance. He also appeared to be thanking her for messages she had passed to him on a similar theme. So had Doris herself been acting as a channel for advice from the spirit world? Haig wasn't explicit on the matter, but the thread of his letter suggests that this was a distinct possibility. It's clear that during the war Doris bombarded him with notes and suggestions, attended séances and took a keen interest in his life at the front. She took Douglas's status and her own very seriously and was anxious that her husband emerge from the war as a public hero. If the spirits could help him to achieve that, so much the better.

What is more remarkable about the messages Haig received is that on the surface he seemed to have little interest in formal religion. George Duncan, Church of Scotland minister in France during the war who met the Commander-in-Chief many times, wrote later that he could not remember Haig ever having mentioned the word 'God' on any public occasion, nor did he bring up matters of religion in private conversation. In contrast, we know that he was in receipt of a constant stream of letters and advice allegedly from the spirit world, courtesy not only of family members but mediums both known and strangers to him. He later wrote that he received several such missives every week for the whole duration of the war. However, Haig was unlikely to have broadcast the fact that he was getting help from the land of the dead. It would hardly have been expected of a military leader that he was being guided by advice from beyond the grave. Even if that advice came from a general of genius.

On 6 January 1916 Haig's sister Henrietta wrote to him with a message from Napoleon whose spirit had been in contact with that of their dead brother George on the astral plane. She told him that the French general was always beside him to advise him, though it's not clear whether she meant that Haig was already the beneficiary of Napoleon's advice or whether the phantom general was about to influence him in subtle ways. Henrietta repeated the message that the angels of Heaven were on Haig's side and that he was God's instrument in defeating the Germans. A few months later, in July, Henrietta, on the same theme, urged him to be aware of Napoleon's presence and accept his judgement, as the Frenchman in his spirit form could visit the German armies and find out what they were planning.

Of course, it might be suggested that even if spirit messages were being passed to Haig, he didn't take the content too seriously. However, the evidence, however strange, suggests that this was far from being the case. In one instance, a psychic contact, this time from the dead Field Marshal Lord Kitchener, was viewed as so significant that it was taken post-haste from the UK to Haig's headquarters in France. After the war, Haig apparently confirmed that this incident had taken place and explained that he saw it as his duty to consider all advice passed to him, even from the spirit world. He kept all these messages for a year following the conclusion of the war and then apparently destroyed them. It's curious, however, that he bothered with them at all if he thought so little of them. One can sense that he didn't want his reputation sullied by any suggestion that he, in prosecuting the war, had relied on advice from the dead, no matter how great their reputations.

But another little known incident suggests that Haig was more than susceptible to strange ideas. A sergeant in the British army convinced Haig that he had invented a 'death ray' which would destroy whole swathes of German troops and artillery. It was several weeks before Haig realised that he was quite simply being fooled.

5

A Legion of Mystics

Many well-known Scots have been influenced by the occult. But there are those who have played a different part in the history of the paranormal, men and women whose roles have been as channels for, and symbols of, that mysterious phenomenon we call the supernatural. There are several such figures whose names echo across the centuries, and those of more recent vintage who will surely find a place in the history of our country.

Merlin

Scots have earned a reputation for being hard headed, but alongside runs a fascination with the supernatural. In fact, Scotland can boast a continuous line of individuals whose mystic abilities have had a worldwide impact, from the distant, almost mythical world of Merlin to the twenty-first century's Gordon Smith whose clientele has included some of the most famous names in the land.

A long tradition links Merlin to Scotland. Detailed investigation by Adam Ardrey published in his book *Finding Merlin* has, the author claims, even pinpointed the site where

Merlin and King Arthur

he once lived. This can be found at the top of the hill in Glasgow where Ardrery Street now stands. Evidence suggests that Merlin was a real person, originally known as Myrddin. His sister, Languoreth (also known as Gwenydd), was married to Rhydderch, ruler of the Kingdom of Strathclyde from 580 to 612 AD. As recounted in Chapter One, Merlin, according to legend, played an important role in the life of King Arthur and was active during a period of turmoil in Scottish history. It was also a time when Christianity was challenging and overcoming pagan sects like the druids.

Intense fighting erupted across the whole of lowland Scotland. Thousands were killed in long forgotten engagements. But one stands out, the Battle of Arderydd in 573 AD – possibly fought to capture Caerlaverlock Castle near Dumfries – which involved different factions within the Strathclyde Kingdom. A civil war of its time. Merlin witnessed the slaughter of many of his relatives, including, by some accounts, three of his sons. After the event Merlin famously 'went mad' and spent several years in the Caledonian Forest in the Borders. Exactly what went on during his time there is a mystery. Many confusing and contradictory accounts have come down to us. In one it is said that it was only during this time in the woods that he gained the power of prophecy and an ability to communicate with animals. Another has it that he appeared at a wedding riding a stag, tore off its antlers and threw them at the bridegroom who was killed. It is difficult, looking back, to decide what is fact and what is invention, but it is clear that Merlin was seen as first and foremost a man with paranormal ability. More than any other figure, he represents the influence of the supernatural on our everyday world.

It might be argued that whether Merlin existed or not is irrelevant. His memory lives on regardless. In the area once covered by the Caledonian Forest, between Peebles and Dumfriesshire, there are several places linked to Merlin. On Hart Fell you will find Merlin's Cave where the magician passed time communing with the spirits of nature and working up spells. It was also a useful place to survey the heavens and reckon from the position of the stars what the future might hold. A few miles away lies Drumelzier, a spot that perhaps deserves greater recognition as it has a long tradition as the site of Merlin's death. A standing stone located where the Drumelzier Burn, now diverted, used to flow into the River Tweed marks the spot.

Merlin, as the archetypal mystic died, the three-fold death. It's an end full of pagan symbolism which it is hard now for us to fully understand. And accounts of how he died vary. According to one he was beaten and stoned by shepherds. As he slipped into the River Tweed he was impaled on fishermen's stakes and drowned at the same time. It's possible that any reference to the involvement of shepherds is a later addition as the link between shepherds and Christianity, Jesus and his flock, is obvious. The sentiment here could be of the new religion overcoming the old. The part played by the fishermen's stakes could, arguably, be a part of the same idea as the fish symbol which was adopted by Christians and is still used today. However, it's more complicated, as the fish was also an important symbol in pagan belief. This is best seen in the figure of the mysterious Fisher King, a guardian of the Otherworld in pre-Christian belief, he became in Christian accounts the protector of the Holy Grail, the vessel in which the blood of Christ was collected as he lay dying on the cross. Maybe the descriptions of Merlin's death are meant to suggest that Christianity had not simply defeated the pagans, but absorbed them and their ideas into the new religion.

This also may explain why a figure like St Kentigern, one of the most important Christians of the sixth century, is pictured with Merlin on a stained-glass window of Stobo Church in the Borders. It's an ancient kirk, part of which is built on the foundations of a seventh century cell linked to St Kentigern. The window pictures St Kentigern standing with his hand raised over a kneeling, long-haired, half naked Merlin, the magician in his 'madman' phase.

The influence of Merlin on literature has been significant, from ancient tales, through the medieval romances of the Round Table and the Grail legends, to modern books, films and cartoons. Less well known is the part his memory played in Scottish history.

Merlin the prophet and seer continued to be referred to centuries after his death. During the Wars of Independence in the thirteenth and fourteenth centuries his alleged predictions were still being used to prophesy victory for one side or the other. According to Sir Walter Scott, a fervent Tory, Merlin had even predicted the union of England and Scotland. But maybe his prophecies are seen as less relevant in the twenty-first century. However, we can be sure that the name of Merlin, because of the enchanted world it represents, will live forever in our minds.

Michael Scott

Scots seem to have an awareness and a tradition that the world of everyday reality sits close to the worlds beyond. There's a veil that separates one from the other, but that can easily be pulled open by those with a certain ability. The Highlands abound with tales of second sight, but the Lowlands too can lay claim to several key psychics, and though Merlin inhabits the land where myth and fact are hard to separate, we are on firmer ground with the 'wizard' Michael Scott. There's no doubt that here we are dealing with a person who lived and left documented proof of his existence.

He was born in Blawearie on the Ettrick Water and lived at Oakwood Tower near Selkirk in the thirteenth century. It seems that he was a man interested in religion, philosophy and science. Like many intellectual Scots of the era who wished to advance their learning he went to Europe to study. Here, it seems, he became famous for his investigation of arcane subjects, although it's not clear whether this included alchemy or those areas described as the black arts. But if it was all above board, as some have argued, it's hard to understand why he earned an international reputation as a powerful magician.

A description by Patrick Tytler, though, dating from the nineteenth century, neatly sums up the reputation that had attached itself to Scott:

> The apparatus of his laboratory, the oriental costume worn by the astrologers of the times, and the appearance of the white-haired and venerable sage as he sat on the roof of his tower observing the face of the heavens and conversing with the stars, were all amply sufficient to impress the minds of the vulgar with awe and terror.

Scott was clearly involved in some kind of investigation into the mysteries of life which might well have involved spells and potions.

Superhuman feats were ascribed to him. It is said that he split the Eildon Hills in the Borders into three so that they look as they do at present. This was done in concert with the Devil, who it is said Scott had the ability to conjure up at will. He is also said to have built Glenluce Abbey in Dumfriesshire overnight. There were more personal encounters. At Drumochter in

Inverness-shire, as he was walking with two friends, the group was attacked by a dragon. Scott's friends fled, but he stayed and slew the beast with a sword. The dragon was cut into three parts and made into soup. When Scott tasted the soup, he immediately gained a vast trove of magical knowledge and the ability to communicate with Satan.

Dragons may or may not have existed. However, in the case of Scott's encounter, the symbolic aspect is quite clear. The dragon was used as a symbol to represent the hidden forces, the magical streams that could be tapped. It also signified the old pagan ideas, as opposed to Christianity. In slaying the dragon and then eating it, Scott had tapped into those forces and been enriched by psychic powers which allowed him to enter realms denied to most. Certainly his contemporaries saw it that way. But it was a legend that lived on for centuries after his death.

The place where in later years he lived and then died, his 'castle' at Oakwood, was regarded as a haunted spot. Children in the Borders would be threatened with a visit by Michael Scott if they did not behave themselves. That literary giant, Sir Walter Scott, and his famous contemporary James Hogg, the Ettrick Shepherd, were fascinated by the legends linked to the 'wizard'. Scott even went to Melrose Abbey to search for the 'wizard's' book of spells that was said to have been buried with him. He incorporated Scott into his novels, as Hogg did in his writings.

Thomas the Rhymer

One question which has fascinated historians is whether Michael Scott and Thomas the Rhymer ever met. Although Scott has earned a fearsome reputation, Thomas is regarded in a rather more kindly fashion as nothing more than a bit of a dreamer. It's not clear why tradition has dealt so differently with these two characters.

As with Michael Scott, Thomas, nicknamed The Rhymer, was undoubtedly a real person. He was a thirteenth-century poet, living between 1210 and 1290, who had gained the ability to see into the future and make predictions of events to come. In a manner similar to that of Michael Scott, Thomas's supernatural ability came through contact with entities from another world – in Thomas's case, a meeting with and abduction by the Queen of the Fairies. This encounter took place in the Eildon Hills where Thomas was approached by a lady dressed in green, who then took him away to live with her among the fairies. Thomas passed seven years with these entities and when he was eventually returned to the real world he had acquired an amazing ability to see into the future. It was the prophecies attributed to him that have made his name, though he was also known at the time as a literary man. 'The Romance of Sir Tristrem' is said to be one of his works.

Prophesies, of course, can be controversial. What exactly is meant in a particular prediction? Can it be interpreted in a different way to suit a particular event? As with any prophet, controversy arises, and Thomas's are in no different a category than arguments over what Nostradamus did or did not mean. In Thomas's case, his prophecies did not appear, as far as is known, in written form till the fifteenth century, but in a sense that is irrelevant. Clearly the predictions were circulating for a long period before they appeared in print, and his influence must have been enormous. Almost every major figure during the Wars of Independence was linked to a prophecy made by Thomas. He was said to have predicted Bruce's ascent to the throne of Scotland, Wallace's success and eventual death and the outbreak of the wars with England.

Thomas was certainly regarded as a man with an uncanny ability to visualise the future. His reputation for accuracy must have been high, as it's hard to explain otherwise why it was seen as important to connect him to leading figures. Mystics were obviously taken seriously and formed an important part of a propaganda war. Having the psychics on your side was a useful tool in persuading people of the righteousness of your cause. The other world you could claim was on your side.

Thomas's prophecies, however, did not just cover the era in which he lived. He is claimed to have predicted a wide range of events, including the defeat of the Scots at Flodden in 1513, the union of England and Scotland in 1707, the building of the Forth Bridge in 1890 and even that the Haig family, of whisky and World War I fame, would reoccupy their old 'seat' at Bemersyde in the Borders. Did The Rhymer predict that Scotland would regain its independence? It's hard to believe that a prophesy on such an important theme is not in there somewhere as well.

It would be nice to think that Scott and Thomas met. They both lived in Border counties, Michael at Aikwood and Thomas at Heslington, not so far apart. There's no evidence that they did, however, but perhaps even Thomas, who comes across as a gentle individual, felt that Scott's reputation was too fearsome even for him, no matter they shared a common interest.

Daniel Home

There's a surprising gap before Scottish mystics re-emerged in the nineteenth century as a major force. Why should that be? The main reason must lie in the attitude that developed towards those with paranormal abilities. From being seen as almost a gift from God, the power of prophecy or the ability to contact other worlds came to be regarded as something evil, a product of the black arts and a gift from the Devil. Individuals, however, continued to predict the future and were consulted regularly over what they had seen. Well-known names among the aristocracy thought nothing of visiting seers and Wise Women for a vision of their future and for charms or spells for cures or to do evil to others. The mystics did not go away, but they were walking a thin line. The Witchcraft Acts of the sixteenth century placed anyone who became too well known for enchantment in a situation where their life could be at risk. Those whose reputations marked them out became victims accused of evil practices and likely to be put to death. It's understandable that any sensible mystic would choose to keep his or her head down.

In another age, Ritchie Graham, who was consulted by many leading people of the sixteenth century, might have been venerated as Thomas the Rhymer had been in his day. As it was, as the most prominent 'magician' of his era, he was imprisoned and executed. The full extent of his influence on the politics of Scotland remains to be fully explored; however, his involvement with the Earl of Bothwell and the treason plot on the life of James VI has earned him a place in history.

But not all sorcerers shared Ritchie's fate. The Countess of Huntly, a contemporary of Mary Queen of Scots, was well known as a witch and regularly consulted local seers to advance her family's interests. Perhaps her aristocratic status saved her from arrest, although other well-connected individuals were put on trial. In 1479 the Earl of Mar was accused of trying to kill his brother James III by witchcraft while, in 1537, Lady Glamis was burned alive for the crime of using magic charms to threaten the life of James V, so position alone was no protection against the witch hunters if it involved treason.

It was not till the nineteenth century, with witchcraft now viewed as mere superstition, that mystics emerged from the shadows. And when they did it was a Scot whose reputation outshone them all.

Daniel Home can lay claim to being one of the world's most famous mediums. He is regarded as an icon by modern psychics who see him as an outstanding example of those who make it their business to bridge the gap between this world and that inhabited by spirits of the dead. Home, however, was capable of more than contacting the phantoms of the departed. He could float through the air and affect objects at a distance without touching them. His ability to make things move simply by looking at them was tested by Sir William Crookes, a famous scientist of the nineteenth century with many achievements to his credit, including the discovery of the element thallium. Crookes published his finding, stating that, having conducted experiments with the medium in his laboratory, he could confirm that Home was genuine. He could do the seemingly impossible and move items by the power of sight alone. Immediately, a storm of publicity broke and Crookes was attacked by other scientists who refused to believe that Home was other than a fraud, no matter what evidence Crookes released to support his claims. Faced with the end of his career as a scientist, Crookes called a halt to his experiments with Home, but did not retract his statements about Home's amazing abilities.

Daniel Home was born in 1833 in Currie, then a village a few miles from the city of Edinburgh. Though his family lived in humble circumstances they, in a way, had a claim to fame. Home's father boasted that he was an illegitimate son of the aristocratic Home family of the Scottish Borders, one of whose members, Sir Alec Douglas Home, became Prime Minister in 1963. According to Home's father, his mother, a servant, had

had an illicit affair with one of the Earl of Home's sons, and Daniel was the end result. Daniel Home certainly believed the story, adding the middle name Dunglas, as a sign of his aristocratic origins. His pretensions have been laughed at by his enemies, but Home asserted that his father had received financial support from the Home family in recognition of the connection. It's a claim, however, that has never been proved.

As a young boy, Home faced a future with no great prospects. But it was at this early age that the ability which would later propel him into the palaces of kings and emperors and the company of famous politicians and writers, emerged. He began to have visions of events that were happening miles away. As early as four years old he saw and reported to his aunt, who he was living with in the Portobello district of Edinburgh, the death of a young cousin long before the news arrived to confirm the tragedy. Voices could also be heard coming from his bedroom when there was no one else there.

It may come as no surprise to learn that Home later explained that his mother, from the Highlands, was herself a seer and that it was from her that he had inherited his psychic ability. But had Home remained in Scotland, perhaps he would not have had the opportunity, at this period, to become the world's most famous medium. At the age of nine, in 1842, his family immigrated to the United States where soon after the country was swept by a passion for Spiritualism.

The craze had been started by the Fox sisters in the town of Rochester in the state of New York. The girls had discovered that they could contact the dead by having the spirits rap out answers on tables or other furniture. It was a basic means of communicating with the departed and Home, by comparison, was capable of far more. He could not only see but speak directly with the spirits of the dead. Even though still a teenager, Home was soon recognised as possessing a special ability and became the darling of wealthy patrons in the state of New York where he lived.

Home, however, was anxious to return to Britain, which he did in 1855. It was a gamble, but one that paid off for Home. Within a decade he was the most famous medium in the world. How did he achieve such fame? According to sceptics, he was simply a brilliant fraudster, but to believers he was simply the most amazing medium of the age. Reports of his séances include some astonishing feats, with plenty of witnesses to confirm the events.

One of his most famous and controversial demonstrated an ability that simply defied the known physical laws of science. At the apartment of the Earl of Dunraven, Ashley House in the Victoria suburb of London, in front of a group that included members of the House of Lords, Home elongated his body so that he grew both longer and thinner. He then floated through an open window, measured at eighteen inches wide and hovered over the street outside some thirty feet up before floating back into the flat through another window. Utterly impossible, but those who saw this bizarre performance signed an affidavit confirming what had happened. They were even willing to describe publicly what they had seen. One of those present, Lord Adare, published an account of the event and could offer no explanation of how Home achieved the feat.

Sir David Brewster, Scotland's foremost scientist, admitted to being amazed by Home's psychic ability and encouraged others to investigate the medium and test him. Sir William Crookes did just that and believed that he had demonstrated that Home possessed unexplained abilities, including that of making musical instruments play without touching them and changing the weight of objects simply by looking at them. He also wrote of how Home materialised a glowing hand which put a piece of shining crystal into Crooke's palm, and confirmed that he had watched Home float from the ground at will. Crookes turned himself into a laughing stock.

However, it all served to bolster Home's reputation, and he was invited to conduct séances for the Tsar of Russia, Napoleon III of France and Queen Sophie of the Netherlands. He was undeniably on first-name terms with the upper classes in Britain, but a question mark hangs over whether he was consulted by Prince Albert and Queen Victoria. Spiritualist circles claimed that he was, but there has never been any conclusive evidence discovered to date to confirm it.

Home had a huge influence in convincing people of importance that the supernatural was not a fantasy and that the spirits of the dead were all around us. Politicians were certainly among those present at his séances, and countless messages from the departed were received by Home and passed on. It's a potentially huge area for investigation and one of the problems has been that Home's success was such that he generated equally determined enemies. Home's repeated offers to scientists that he would welcome their investigation of his strange abilities were simply rejected. With a career to lose, scientists steered clear of involvement with the paranormal. They had seen what had happened to William Crookes when he had put his head above the parapet. Disillusioned, Home turned his back on the scientific community. But his reputation was such that attacks on his credibility continue to the present.

One can sense that Home became gradually disillusioned with his aim of bringing reassurance to the living that death was not the end. He published two books describing his many experiences. They were, of course, slated by the critics.

A constant throughout his life was his pride in his Scottish roots. On his death in 1886, his wife gave £4,000 to Edinburgh City Council to erect a statue to Home in the form of a fountain which stood for many years outside the Canongate Church. The remnants of this sculpture can now be found in the Edinburgh College of Parapsychology.

Home may be long dead, but the legacy he left lives on. In his book *Spirit Messenger*, Scotland's best-known present day medium Gordon Smith pays tribute to Home and this reflects the general feeling of psychics towards the Edinburgh seer, that he was a medium with worldwide influence.

Helen Duncan

During the nineteenth century, the supernatural reasserted itself as a subject people could involve themselves in, could practise and as a topic for investigation. Many psychics sprang up, claiming all sorts of abilities, and many of their names have been lost in the mists of time. But one stands out, that of Helen Duncan, whose career as a psychic came to the attention of a British Prime Minister and whose activities were seen as a threat to national security.

Helen Duncan was born in the village of Callander, bordering the Trossachs, in 1897. From an early age she revealed an ability to see things hidden to others and with prompting from her husband, Henry, she participated in séances organised by the spiritualist movement and soon had a well-established reputation. Helen was also a 'physical' medium. In other words, she produced ectoplasm from her body which then formed itself into the spirits of the dead to allow them to walk among and speak to the living.

As Helen's reputation grew so sceptics, which included some active spiritualists, set out to expose her. In January 1933 at a séance held at 24 Stafford Street, Edinburgh, it was claimed that Helen was caught using a stuffed object which she had pretended was the spirit of a dead child, Little Peggy. On 3 May 1933 Helen was charged at Edinburgh Sheriff Court with 'pretending that she was a medium through whom the spirits of deceased persons were openly materialised to become visible to and converse with those present in the room with her'. To put it bluntly, Helen was a fake. The case went against her and Helen was fined ten pounds.

But if her enemies thought that that was the end of Helen Duncan they could not have been more wrong. The trial attracted worldwide attention and Helen was catapulted into celebrity status. And while she had her detractors, she could also boast determined supporters convinced of Helen's ability to communicate with the dead. There had been a long list of witnesses who had spoken up for her at her trial. Helen was more in demand than ever. But as her reputation grew it became more difficult to live in the shadows, as she was soon to find out to her cost.

The outbreak of World War II in 1939 in one way pushed interest in the supernatural to one side. Day to day matters became pressing and with them less time available for people to immerse themselves in outside interest, no matter how fascinating. But on the other hand, the death of sons and daughters and husbands created a strong desire to make contact with them in any way possible. In many cases too, the exact nature of the victim's death was not clear. Secrecy was at a premium and the circumstances under which members of the armed forces had lost their lives were not revealed or, often, were simply not known.

Mediums with their access to the spirit world were seen as a way to find out the fate of those killed or missing. It was into this information vacuum that Helen Duncan was to step with unforeseen consequences.

There's no doubt that by 1944 Helen was one of Britain's

best-known mediums who was in demand across the country. In January of that year Helen was active in the south of England in the town of Portsmouth, giving séances at a psychic centre known as the Master Temple. But why on the nineteenth of that month did police turn up at Helen's meeting? Why Helen should have been targeted in this way has never been satisfactorily explained, as psychics in many cities were relaying messages from the dead and many well-known people were making use of mediums in an effort to discover what had happened to missing servicemen or to find out more about the way they had died. Furthermore, by 1944 the allies were well on top in the war against Germany, and it could only be a matter of time before the war was won. So why take action against Helen Duncan at this time? The immediate result of the police presence at Helen's séance was that she was arrested by Detective Sergeant Fred Ford for falsely claiming that she could tell fortunes. But technically, on the face of it, that was not what she had been doing; she had been, as was her normal practice, communicating with the dead

The next bizarre development was a decision to put Helen Duncan on trial at London's famous Old Bailey court. If the government had wanted to generate publicity for Helen they could not have tried harder. Did they deliberately set out to do so for some unknown reason? When the papers splashed details of the trial across front pages, Prime Minister Winston Churchill reportedly exploded in fury and on 3 April 1944 dictated an irate memo to the then Home Secretary Herbert Morrison, demanding to know 'why the Witchcraft Act of 1735 was used in a modern Court of Justice'. It's a question many raised at the time and since.

It seems that Helen had breached secrecy without being aware of it. Portsmouth was an important seaport with a key role during World War II. It was also assumed that Nazi spies were active in the city and there was worry that classified information might make its way back to Germany and compromise allied action. The planned invasion of Normandy, set for June 1944, was of special concern. But, as far as is known, Helen had not revealed anything relative to the proposed D-Day landings.

The episode in contention concerned one of her séances, when a spirit had 'come through' wearing a sailor's uniform, including a cap bearing the inscription *H.M.S. Barham*. He had, according to Helen, sat beside a woman in the audience and said, 'Sorry, darling. My ship went down in the Med. I've crossed to the other side.' His girlfriend, to whom the sailor had spoken, was distraught, as she had had no news of her boyfriend. His death came as a complete shock. The following day she rang the Admiralty asking if it was true. In fact, the spirit Helen had contacted had spoken the truth, but the navy was keeping the fate of the *Barham*, blown up by a German U-boat, a secret. It was government policy not to reveal the sinking of British warships in order to keep the Nazi hierarchy ignorant of their successes – even to the extent of deceiving the British relatives of dead sailors. The unfortunate girlfriend was sworn to secrecy. But military intelligence now had Helen in their sights.

There's no evidence that Helen was ever considered to be a German spy, only that she might be leaking secret information. However, in charging Helen under the Witchcraft Act, there were plenty at the time who thought they were using the proverbial hammer to crack a walnut. It might be asked reasonably, why not just ignore it? Portsmouth was full of sailors and those connected with naval operations. Several hundred sailors were killed in the *Barham* disaster, even more survived. How long could the sinking of a British destroyer be kept secret in these circumstances? And, in any case, who was listening to Helen Duncan? Was it likely German spies would be attending her séances where, in any case, they would soon be found out?

It all suggests that there is far more to the Helen Duncan case than meets the eye. The use of psychics as part of modern warfare is now well known. Both the former Soviet Union and the USA conducted experiments with mediums, particularly in relation to remote viewing, the ability to see and describe objects at a distance. It would certainly give a military advantage over an enemy. But that's only one part of wider and even more bizarre research that was conducted. As described in the book *Men who Stare at Goats*, tests were carried out to judge whether animals could be killed simply by looking at them. The British government have always been coy over its involvement in similar experiments, but the UK intelligence agencies have an obsession with secrecy on a par with almost any country in the world. Admission of any connection with psychic testing will be a long time in leaking out. But it can't be dismissed, as the upper echelons of British society have a long-standing interest in the paranormal, and Winston Churchill was certainly one of those who had his own brushes with the supernatural, so is it possible that Helen, one of the best-known mediums of the day, had been consulted by the government about wartime activities?

The most obvious possibility is in relation to Adolf Hitler, who was believed to have been influenced by astrology and predictions of future events. Other leading Nazis were known to have an active interest in the power of magic. No evidence has presented itself in government files released to the public, it's true, but a mine of information relating to wartime activities remains buried within time-protected vaults.

Helen's possible link to the government may explain why

Churchill was so enraged by her prosecution. No doubt the intention of putting her on trial was to force her to keep quiet, but it had the opposite effect, making her better known than ever. It raised both her profile and her credibility, neither of which had been the intended outcome. And those who would dismiss the suggestion that Helen had assisted the government, and it was all, as Churchill himself announced, 'tomfoolery', have to explain why Helen Duncan was systematically followed by government agencies right into the 1950s. As late as October 1956, a séance held by Helen in Edinburgh was raided by police. Her death came a few weeks later, and with her died many questions that will only be answered with the release of more government files.

Robert Kirk

By the time of Helen's death, strange, previously unknown phenomena were hitting the headlines, Unidentified Flying Objects (UFOs) and alien abductions. In fact, neither was new – strange objects had been reported over the skies of Scotland for centuries and abduction by entities from other worlds had a long history. In past ages, fairies were the main culprits. They would capture individuals, Thomas the Rhymer being one of the best known, and take them to the land of Fairy, often a place below the ground, where he or she would be kept prisoner for many years. It could certainly be dismissed as a bit of a tale, fables from a distant past.

But the Reverend Robert Kirk, Minister at Aberfoyle in the Trossachs during the seventeenth century, changed all that. He has probably had a greater effect on modern belief in the supernatural than any other figure. The contemporary obsession with alien abduction, in the eyes of some, can be traced back to the claims made by Kirk in his 1691 publication, *The Secret Commonwealth of Elves, Fauns and Fairies*. It was a slender volume but had a big impact, which has rippled down to the present day.

Little is known about Robert Kirk, though his grave can be seen in the churchyard just outside Aberfoyle. You can also visit the fairy mound close by where Kirk claims to have on many occasions encountered the fairy people. His documentation of their characteristics and actions in *The Secret Commonwealth* reads more like a PhD thesis than some fanciful account. According to Kirk, the fairies had fires which burned without wood or coal and lights with no obvious power source. They wore clothes just like those of humans, and they spoke the language of the country in which they lived. In fact, they looked like men and women. They had doctors and nurses, got married and had children. The main difference between man and fairy was in the nature of their bodies. Those of the fairies were of a different nature and were not solid. This allowed them to pass through hard matter and enter buildings without being seen, a claim that echoes the ability of contemporary aliens, as reported by today's witnesses.

Robert Kirk's account is seen as a bridge between traditional beliefs and those of modern times. Debate has raged over whether he encountered astral beings or alien entities. Although the assumption has been that aliens come from outer space, some abductees have reported being taken to underground locations, just as it is reported fairies did in past times. Whatever the reality of Kirk's experience, the details he recorded have been used across the world as proof of the existence of entities that remain invisible to most human beings.

★   ★   ★

The Brahan Seer

In the same way, the prophecies of the Brahan Seer have been viewed as on a par with those of Nostrodamus in confirming the ability of certain individuals to see into the future. So who was the Brahan Seer? In fact, it is not one individual but several, the Brahan Seer is a title and not a name, and there is no process of choosing who holds the title. It is given as the seer proves an ability to prophesy or see events happening far away that they could not have known by normal means. On the Isle of Skye, Alexander Macleod was lying in bed on 16 April 1746 when he heard a voice calling to him, 'The prince is defeated'. The downfall of Charles Edward Stuart at the battle of Culloden, many miles away, had been revealed to him long before any message could arrive. Macleod was not a mystic and this, for him, was a one-off event, but it was the type of incident which, repeated often enough, would establish a man's reputation as a visionary.

The best-known Brahan Seer was Kenneth Orr, who lived in the seventeenth century and was born near Uig on the Isle of Lewis. It is said that he worked for Kenneth Mackenzie, the third Earl of Seaforth, laird not only of Lewis, but much of Ross-shire. Orr's predictions were recorded by Alexander Mackenzie, but not written down till many years after the medium had died. His book, *The Prophecies of the Brahan Seer*, did not in fact appear till 1878. Some have argued that Mackenzie, who was a folklorist, was out to make a reputation for himself and invented or at least 'improved' the predictions made by Kenneth Orr. That may or may not be the case. However, whatever the truth, what is undeniable is that the prophecies are still scrutinised today. The one that has caught attention in recent years is that dealing with black rain. It runs: 'Sheep shall eat men, men will eat sheep, the black rain will eat all things. In the end, old men will return from new lands'. 'Black rain' has been interpreted as a reference to the discovery of oil and the rise of the oil industry, which now dominates the north east economy. And 'sheep shall eat men' could refer to the earlier Highland clearances, when families were removed from their land to make way for sheep. There are more specific predictions that have been linked to the building of the Caledonian Canal and prophesying all kinds of disasters.

Orr earned his reputation as a seer from an early age. His mother gave him a magic stone which had been passed to her by a phantom claiming to be the daughter of a long dead king of Norway. Kenneth took possession of the stone at the age of seven and from then on experienced many visions. It earned him a reputation and influence, but also brought about his downfall. Tradition has it that when the Earl of Seaforth was sent on a diplomatic mission to Paris, his wife, the Countess, asked the Brahan Seer to describe to her how her husband was passing his time there. Eventually, he told her that the Earl was involved with another woman. She had him executed for his impudence. As he was taken to his death, Orr predicted that the Seaforth inheritance and those of related clans would 'pass to strangers', a prophesy which has in many ways been fulfilled.

But the idea that Scotland should have a Brahan Seer lives on. The latest linked to the title was Swein Macdonald, who was born in 1931 in Elgin and spent some time in Glasgow before, following an accident, taking up crofting on Kincardine Hill overlooking the Dornoch Firth. I met him there in the 1990s. His second sight, he believed, was inherited most probably through his father, but it is said that his mother also possessed this gift.

In Swein there was a formidable combination of psychic talent. He was said to have predicted many significant events, including the outbreak of the Falklands War in 1982 and the assassination of Lord Mountbatten in 1979. However, he also gave many predictions of an individual nature and claimed he was in touch with many famous people. It's true that he was well known in the United States where his reputation for accuracy was well established. In fact, Swein Macdonald may well have been better known abroad than he was in Scotland.

But maybe that is because Scotland had produced, and continues to produce, so many outstanding mediums. I have met several, including Glasgow's Gary Gray and the late Ray Tod, who was an outstanding physical medium. Ray Tod lived and died in obscurity in spite of his astonishing talent. Gordon Smith, however, originally from Glasgow, has continued the tradition of those Scottish mediums who earn a huge reputation. He is as well known today as Daniel Home was in the nineteenth century.

And, in keeping with many top mediums, Gordon Smith became aware of his psychic ability at an early age. In his book *Spirit Messenger*, he describes an extraordinary meeting with a woman at a top Glasgow hotel, a lady who was desperate to consult Gordon because of his fast-growing reputation as an exceptional medium. She made a strange request. Her husband was a person of influence and she was worried that he was about to be engulfed by a public scandal. Would Gordon ask the spirits to work on people so that her husband's reputation was saved? Gordon Smith explained that this was not the way the spirit world worked. He could not get them to intervene simply on request.

But, in noting this incident, we have, in a sense, come full circle. Merlin, in the distant past, surely found himself in situations where similar requests were made to him, as have many psychics no doubt since. The desire by those in important positions to consult with other worlds and gain an advantage by doing so, appears to be an ever-present factor in the history of Scottish society.

6

The Supernatural in War and Peace

The impact of the supernatural is still with us. The career of Donald Dewar, Scotland's first First Minister, demonstrates that the paranormal is not a phenomenon that exists only in the past, but is in fact an ever-present aspect of life in Scotland. Charles Rennie Mackintosh may have been a designer, Ramsay MacDonald a politician and Hugh Dowding a war leader, but what links them is the role that the world beyond played in influencing their lives.

Charles Rennie Mackintosh

In October 2011 it was reported that a ghost, taken to be that of Charles Rennie Mackintosh, had appeared at Hill House in Helensburgh, one of his most famous architectural commissions. The alleged presence of this phantom might be less surprising to those aware of the mystical side to Mackintosh's character. In truth, it's only recently that the influence of mysticism on his work and that of Margaret, his wife, with whom he closely collaborated, has been openly recognised. That may be partly due to the fact that for many years after his death, Mackintosh's reputation languished in obscurity. Even in his lifetime, he was not famous in his homeland, and he died in 1928 a forgotten man. Indeed, he would probably have been astonished to learn that he would become to future generations the icon he is today.

Charles Rennie Mackintosh was born in June 1868 in Glasgow's Parson Street, but when he was six years old moved to Firpark Terrace in Dennistoun. In view of the mystical nature of his work, it was a fitting address, situated so close to the Cathedral and the hill of the Necropolis, sites of the very origins of the city, an area inhabited by druids and then taken over by that strange character St Mungo as the basis for propagating his odd brand of Christianity tinged with more than a hint of paganism.

And perhaps Mackintosh was marked from the beginning for a life infused with mysticism. He was born with a clubbed foot, which by tradition was believed to indicate one who had been marked by the Devil. It brought with it abilities out of the ordinary, but, coming from the dark side, had a two-edged tinge. It was a gift that was cursed. Mackintosh's father was a superintendent in the city's police force, and, it has been suggested, an active Freemason. Whether or not the craft influenced Mackintosh's ideas is unclear. However, Mackintosh's earliest known architectural work was a tomb with a Celtic theme he designed in 1888 for the then recently deceased Chief Constable, Alexander McCall. The monument which still stands in the Glasgow Necropolis may not be typically Mackintosh, but it's a clear pointer to the mystical influence evident in his later, better known work.

It's not clear why Mackintosh was attracted to architecture, though he revealed an artistic inclination from an early age. He served his apprenticeship in the office of the architect John

Hutchinson while attending evening classes at the Glasgow School of Art, where he came to the attention of the college director, Francis Newbery. Mackintosh, however, continued his architectural work at the firm of Honeyman & Keppie, though all the while developing his interest in designing a range of materials, including furniture and room interiors.

In 1900 he married the artist Margaret Macdonald. It has been argued that it was their fusion of ideas and personalities that unlocked the mystical part of Mackintosh. However, although their union and her style undoubtedly influenced Mackintosh's creative ability, he was producing works tinged with mysticism several years before they finally tied the knot.

His 1892 painting, 'The Harvest Moon', still puzzles and intrigues. It is referred to as 'symbolic', which may be one way of saying that even the art experts don't fully understand it. And it is difficult to unravel what message Mackintosh was trying to convey. It was undeniably spiritual, as its central focus is a female figure that appears to be a representation of an angel standing in front of a pale yellow orb, the moon. The angel's wings encircle the moon and together they sit at the top of a tree, which may well represent the Tree of Life. The upper half of the picture is painted in a hypnotic blue tinged with purple. The overall image of the painting is one of mystery. Whatever levels of meaning Mackintosh included within it, he definitely meant to convey the idea of the influence of the feminine on the world, an influence which may go unnoticed but is nonetheless all pervasive in its impact. And the female, too, can be seen as representing the unknown and the unknowable, the supernatural aspect to human existence. Not only in 'The Harvest Moon' has Mackintosh placed a female figure at the heart of the painting, but she is represented against the background of the moon, that archetypal, and age-old symbol of female influence. The blue background not only represents the sky, but the enchanted world of mystery. In Scottish folklore it was a colour, as much as the better known green, which was linked to the supernatural. Charles was to return to the symbolism of the feminine time and time again in his art and design work.

Mackintosh had some strange obsessions. In a letter in 1933, Professor Thomas Bryce reported a visit Mackintosh paid to his anatomy laboratory in 1893, where he asked to examine under a microscope the developing eye of a fish. 'He at once', wrote the professor, 'sketched it and incorporated it into the decorative design' for Queen Margaret's Medical College. What the professor did not perhaps fully appreciate was the mystical significance of the fish eye motif. If you visit Malta, for example, you will find painted on the trawlers there a fish-shaped eye. It is intended to ward off evil spirits and protect against harm. The all-seeing eye is, of course, well known from the times of ancient Egypt down to the present as a protective charm, but as a symbol in the form of a fish's eye it is probably less popular.

The period that Mackintosh was working in experienced what is known as a Celtic revival, a renewed interest in the myths and legends of the distant past, but it was also an era that saw the rise of secret societies, including those of a magical bent such as the Order of the Golden Dawn and the internationally active Rosicrucians. There has been speculation as to the extent of the influence these developments had on Mackintosh. There's no evidence that he joined the Rosicrucians, but his mentor at Glasgow School of Art, the man who encouraged his art, Francis Newbery, was apparently a member of the Order. The Rosicrucians were particularly active during the 1890s and early part of the twentieth century, holding a number of exhibitions, including one in Brussels in 1891. Mysticism was certainly the flavour of the day, and it would be surprising if

Mackintosh had not caught a whiff of it. In fact, his artwork, certainly in conjunction with his wife Margaret's, suggests that the theme of the supernatural played a big part in his and her professional life.

A good example is a painting by Margaret Mackintosh of a baby in a rose. A rose is a symbolic womb, but it is capable of various levels of meaning, which is why it is an emblem adopted by many secret societies. It can represent life, rebirth and a link with the other world. Its frequent use by Charles may also hint at a connection to the Rosicrucians. Although the origins of the name are disputed, one theory is that it represents the fusion of the words 'rose' and 'cross'. A rose, of course, is also a symbol which represents femininity. However, neither Charles nor Margaret Mackintosh were arguing for some form of proto-feminism. What they were aiming to represent through their work was the balance of life forces, the combination of male and female elements. As in the now well-known theory of Eastern mysticism, the yin and yang of life, which together, it is argued, make for a more balanced and fulfilling existence.

Their attempts to inject this symbolism into their work between 1902 and 1904 can be viewed in Hill House. Here Charles made extensive use of squares, which appear throughout the building on furniture, decoration and even as window shapes. Why is this motif so pervasive? The square in mystical geometric symbolism stands for a man and masculinity. A circle, by contrast, represents a woman and femininity. In the same way colours were also used throughout the couple's work to balance masculine and feminine elements – purple and blue for the male, pink and white for female – symbolism was very much in evidence at Hill House.

The significance of wall decorations in the dining room at Hill House has aroused much controversy. Do they represent no more than a vase, or as some experts have suggested, the stylised naked body of Mackintosh's wife Margaret? The presence of sexual imagery within Mackintosh's work is disputed, though it forms a key part of his art according to some commentators. To take one instance, the writing cabinet in the drawing room of Hill House, the doors of which open to reveal a colourful design of buds and petals, has been viewed as symbolic of female sexuality. A sense of mysticism certainly fills the air of this best-known creation of Mackintosh that can be seen in such examples as the plaster panel described as a willow tree. Mackintosh often incorporated images in this form as a stylised version of the Tree of Life. It's a symbol that predates Christianity, as in the *Yggdrasil* of Norse mythology, the giant ash tree supports the sky and links the world of man to that of the underworld.

His ability to incorporate motifs from across the world within his artistic creations is also evident in the wall decorations he put together for a house at 78 Derngate, Northampton. The design is made up of a series of pyramid shapes which, replicating the design of the Great Pyramid at Giza, are each covered in a gleaming sheath of white. This has long been stripped from the ancient pyramids, but originally they were covered in a layer of marble to make these huge structures glisten in the sun. The Egyptian theme can also be seen in the Mackintosh dining room reconstructed in Glasgow's Hunterian Art Gallery, where there sits a typical long-backed Mackintosh table-chair with a key difference: the headrest is shaped like an enormous eye with a round hole where the pupil would be. It is clearly intended to represent the all-seeing eye symbol of the ancient Egyptians.

For Mackintosh, a building was not an object but a space with a living and vibrant aura. It had an influence on those who lived and worked within it, and so the way the interior was set out, the colours and symbols with which it was decorated, were not chosen by chance, but quite deliberately to create the right atmosphere. The interior of the Glasgow School of Art was not painted as the Glasgow *Evening Times* described it, in 'an artistic shade of green', by chance. Its choice was no accident. It is the supreme colour of the mystical, the sure sign of the other world as shown by the colour of Robin Hood's clothing and the garments worn by the leprechauns of Ireland. Mackintosh was proclaiming that by entering this space you were passing into another dimension where different influences operated, whether you were aware of them or not.

It has been noted by his admirers that Mackintosh made frequent use of green in his work, but he also decorated in other colours with a mystic connection, even in the most unlikely of settings. The *Daily Record* building in Renfrew Lane put up between 1900 and 1904 would not appear an obvious choice as an example of mystic symbolism. However, it did not escape the Mackintosh effect. The facade was made up of glazed white brick interspersed with red and green. Certainly, it creates the stylised image of a tree, and that would be in keeping with the mythological Tree of Life which appears in many of Mackintosh's works, and also, of course, on Glasgow City's coat of arms. But there is more, as Mackintosh made a deliberate choice of the colour scheme. Green represents life and the creative force, while red is the colour of protection, particularly in warding off evil. I would add one factor generally missed in consideration of the *Daily Record* building. In keeping with Mackintosh's interest in Egyptian themes, the top of each Tree of Life is in the triangular shape of a pyramid. One can be sure that the inclusion of this image was not accidental.

Looking back, it appears that Mackintosh was influenced by the writing of Sir Patrick Geddes, the Aberdeenshire botanist turned town planner and sociologist, whose views of city layout had so much influence across the world. Geddes believed in a holistic view of urban living, that the individual interacted with the city to form a greater whole. Geddes had published in 1889 a best-selling book, *The Evolution of Sex*, in which he argued that a man and woman might, by tradition, be opposites, but together they formed a powerful united force.

Geddes and Charles and Margaret Mackintosh formed a friendship from their days as students. Charles surely picked up on Geddes' ideas. The use of black and white, unity through contrast, is an ever-present theme in Mackintosh's work which represents in microcosm the overall effect he aimed to achieve.

It was unfortunate that Mackintosh's genius was not recognised during his lifetime. Although not wholly overlooked, he earned far greater recognition and praise for his innovative achievements abroad than in his home country. Disillusioned and unable to secure commissions for work, Mackintosh spent the last years of his life in France painting watercolours, and died in 1928 in quiet obscurity.

James Ramsay MacDonald

Mackintosh doesn't appear to have been much interested in politics. He did though live to see the election of Britain's first-ever Labour party Prime Minister, a man, as it turned out, with many secrets of his own.

James Ramsay MacDonald was haunted throughout his life by a mystery that was never satisfactorily solved. On his birth certificate his name was recorded as James MacDonald Ramsay, a fact he only discovered in later life. The future Labour Prime Minister had been born out of wedlock and his mother, Anne Ramsay, never married. Ramsay MacDonald never discovered who his father was and his mother never told him. The circumstances of his birth from the start placed him in a world of uncertainty, one in which he, from his early years, perhaps to anchor his life, sought comfort from in the spirit world, an interest encouraged by his mother and one that endured throughout his life. MacDonald's driving force, his will to succeed in the face of enormous obstacles, having been born into poverty and illegitimacy, cannot be properly understood without appreciation that he always felt that the world beyond was close to him and supported him in his career.

Born on 12 October 1866 in a but and ben cottage in Lossiemouth, MacDonald, in spite of his working class roots, is one well-known figure who, one gets the impression, Scots would rather forget. You would be hard put to find any memorials or fond reminiscences of a man who in 1924 became the first ever Labour party Prime Minister. To many on the left of British politics, MacDonald was a traitor, a man who sold out his supporters to form a national government with the Tory party in 1931. He didn't see it that way. Everything he did, all the abuse he suffered, was a part of his mission to save the country. And he knew what had to be done. The spirit world, no less, had confirmed that he was following the right course of action.

From an early age, MacDonald's head was filled with stories of the supernatural. His grandmother, Bella Ramsay, was deeply interested in the legends and myths of the area, and MacDonald, in an age before television, spent many hours listening to tales of the strange beings encountered and unexplained incidents that had involved friends and neighbours. The paranormal was not just history, but an ever-present even for those who, like his grandmother, regularly attended the strictly Presbyterian Free Kirk. There was no disgrace in taking superstition seriously, and Ramsay MacDonald was never embarrassed by his interest in the supernatural, even if he did not talk about it openly.

As he later noted, people in Lossiemouth often reported witnessing the appearance of a 'death candle', a strange light that emerged from the house or cottage where a death would shortly occur. It could even be followed as it made its way purposefully to the nearest kirkyard. Wise women using charms and spells were still active in the area even though the Kirk frowned on the practice. In an age where the danger of childbirth had not been conquered and medicine was basic, individuals continued to look for help to well-established remedies – witchcraft in another age, but in the nineteenth century its practitioners faced no more than censure from the local minister and congregation, criticism which was usually ignored.

MacDonald was certainly fascinated by the survival of ancient beliefs in an age of science and technology. One of the first books he owned as a teenager was Hugh Miller's *My Schools and Schoolmasters*, with its stories of ghosts and phantoms. Miller, with his interest in both the supernatural and in scientific advancement, reflected the mixture of reality and mysticism that would also characterise MacDonald in his political career.

MacDonald is remembered as a noted orator, famous for his brilliant speeches. It was an ability he developed from an early age, regularly taking part in school debates. His earliest known was a speech he gave in September 1883 at the age of seventeen on the subject of superstition, which he described as being 'as common in these times as it ever was'. He condemned 'silly stories' about witchcraft, spectres and prophesy, but that was only to make the point that the supernatural was 'a more real and formidable thing to cultured minds'. In other words, the paranormal had a deeper base and a more pervasive influence on the world than people realised. Tales of ghostly encounters were no more than the froth of an intensive interaction between this world and the other side.

But MacDonald also possessed a practical streak. There was a living to be earned. He was also ambitious, and the drive to succeed could not be satisfied by staying in Lossiemouth, with its limited opportunity for advancement. Circumstances took him in 1885 to Bristol, where he had obtained a post as assistant to a clergyman. For unknown reasons, however, it didn't work out and within a few months MacDonald was back in Lossiemouth once again, looking for an opportunity that would lead to a rewarding career. London beckoned. In Bristol, MacDonald had come into contact with the left-wing activists, including members of the Fabian Society. He realised that, for a man of his background, a future could be found within the budding Labour movement. His rise was rapid. He was an excellent speaker and, as it turned out, a formidable journalist, and in 1906 he was returned as the Member of Parliament for Leicester.

However, within a few years the thrill of success and achievement was to turn sour, and personal tragedies would spark the resurgence of the supernatural as a powerful force in his life. For a period it had all gone so well. In 1896 he married Margaret Ethel Gladstone, the great-niece of the famous scientist Lord Kelvin and daughter of John Gladstone, a founder of the YMCA. Socially, it was a big step up for MacDonald. He had come a long way from the but and ben at Lossiemouth. Unfortunately, the wheel of fate spun, and in February 1910, his four-year-old son David died unexpectedly, probably of diphtheria. MacDonald felt the loss deeply. In September the following year his wife Margaret died, leaving him to look after their five surviving children. These deaths were hammer blows for MacDonald. However, he gained some comfort by sensing that their spirit forms were forever after by his side. He wrote that, 'since he died, my little boy has been my constant companion. He sits with me and I feel his little warm hand in mine'.

It's worth noting that after Margaret's death, MacDonald never remarried. That was because he felt her presence around him all the time. He kept an extensive diary and forever after noted in it on the anniversary of her death exactly where he was at that time. In September 1915 he wrote that he had spent the anniversary alone in a Bristol hotel. He didn't, he explained, like to share his grief with anyone, but recorded that he had been reading 'spiritualist literature', a significant comment in view of his preoccupation with his wife's death. He felt her presence, that she was at his side, but like many people, looked for reassurance from those who could be seen as experts in the field, spiritualist mediums.

And in the years to come he certainly needed Margaret's support from the other side. Without the certainty that she was looking after him, it is hard to believe that he could have survived, mentally and emotionally, the battering his career was about to take. It may be hard to believe now, but for many years MacDonald was vilified for being too left-wing. He opposed the Boer Wars, a stand for which the press and many organisations roundly condemned him. Equally bravely, he was an outspoken critic of Britain's involvement in World War I. This led to years of outright abuse, threats to his life, attempts to ban him from speaking and calls for him to be prosecuted as a traitor. The majority of the Labour Party supported the war and came to view MacDonald as an embarrassment. A man, as they say, with a great career behind him. In the post-war election of 1918 he reaped the whirlwind, losing his seat in Parliament. Even MacDonald believed his political career was at an end.

And so it must have seemed to his colleagues. But within six years, like a reborn Lazarus, MacDonald would not only be elected leader of the Labour party but emerge as the first-ever Labour Prime Minister. How had such a transformation come about? Where had MacDonald gained the strength to carry on?

He undoubtedly believed that he had the spirits of little David and his wife Margaret at his side, but he had also turned to Spiritualism for support. During the disastrous election campaign of 1918 he had recorded in his diary the many occasions when he had seen the spirit form of Margaret as he tramped the streets of Leicester. In April 1919 during a solitary walk on London's Hampstead Heath, he recorded that the phantoms of the dead had joined him as he made his way across the grass. These were not isolated incidents. His involvement with the supernatural was by now on a more established footing.

In November 1925, Dennis Bradley, a well-known spiritualist of the time, wrote to MacDonald, a man who had by then served a period as Prime Minister, enclosing a copy of a book he had written called *The Wisdom of the Gods*. In the letter, Bradley drew MacDonald's attention to page 402 of the publication which, he wrote, contained a short account of the psychic incident they had both experienced. MacDonald did not appear disconcerted in the slightest by the prospect that his involvement with the world of phantoms could become public knowledge. He simply thanked Bradley for the copy of the book which, he said, he would read in due course, as he was busy with other matters at the moment.

Bradley had, as it happens, written to him the previous March, inviting him to attend a séance with an American spiritualist, George Valiantine. Valiantine was a 'direct voice' medium and the best around, according to Bradley. A 'direct voice' medium, as the description suggests, was a psychic through whom the spirits of the departed could speak. It was usually carried out while the medium was in a trance. The simple fact that Bradley wrote to MacDonald suggests, in spite of the attempt by biographers to play it down, that MacDonald was active in spiritualist circles. It's hard to understand why, if not, Bradley would have approached so well known a politician in the first place.

It's hard to avoid the conclusion that MacDonald was 'a man of mystery', as the well-known political activist Beatrice Webb, a founder of the Fabian Society, described him. Particularly strange was his involvement with a club known as the Ark, set up by the aristocratic Lady Londonderry and meeting at her home in London, whose numbers included many of the leading lights of the era. Each member took the name of an entity or animal. Winston Churchill, bizarrely, was known as Winston the Warlock. Lady Londonderry was called Circe, the sorceress who in mythology turned Ulysses' men into pigs. Former Prime Minister Arthur Balfour was known as Arthur the Albatross. MacDonald took the name Hamish the Hart. The Hart is well known as a mystical beast symbolic of many things, including, with its antlers, the cross of Christ. It's hard to believe that MacDonald chose this name by chance. Speculation then as now surrounds the activities of the Ark. Black magic rituals have been suggested, but that, at present, can be no more than guesswork.

We're on firmer ground where MacDonald's contacts with Spiritualism are concerned. In September 1931, the spiritualist medium Mrs Grace Cooke contacted MacDonald, who had by now been Prime Minister on two separate occasions, enclosing a message from Margaret in the spirit world. According to Mrs Cooke, Margaret wanted her husband to know that she was delighted that he was listening to the spiritual forces surrounding him, and that 'she knew all and was' her husband's 'constant helper'. Margaret, Mrs Cooke said in the letter, was standing at his side and 'had a great deal to do' with his decisions.

It's clear that this message not only repeated what Margaret allegedly wanted MacDonald to know, but also what Margaret had told the medium about her interaction with her Prime Minister husband. It's clearly unlikely that Grace Cooke would have written to MacDonald without an awareness that he was both interested in spiritualist messages and that he sensed the presence of his wife's spirit. MacDonald replied within a few days, thanking her for her letter and saying that he was grateful for any message that came his way. It was the start of a lengthy correspondence that continued till MacDonald's death.

The content of these later letters has never been revealed, but they appear to relate to the opinions of his dead wife on his role as leader of the national government from 1931 to 1935. MacDonald served a third term as Prime Minister, but this time with the support of the Tory party. He thought he was doing it for the good of the country, but to the left he was ever after regarded as a traitor to the Labour cause. Without the support of Margaret from the other side, it is doubtful that he would have got through such a difficult period. When he died of a heart attack in November 1937 while on a cruise aboard the liner the *Reina del Pacifico*, it's hard to escape the conclusion that the end brought him a welcome reunion with those he loved.

The dead were always in his company. In 1933, over twenty years after the death of his son David, he wrote, 'I wandered over the Lossiemouth roads holding the hand of my little boy in his dark blue jersey'. Death, in his view, was not a separation. The spirits of the departed could still be there to advise and offer comfort when needed. MacDonald could not have survived without them.

Hugh Dowding

MacDonald may have kept quiet about his interest in Spiritualism, but the same can't be said of Hugh Dowding. It must have been a strange sight, the former leader of the RAF's Fighter Command during the Battle of Britain standing up in the House of Lords and arguing for the repeal of the Witchcraft Act. But then, Hugh Dowding was no ordinary person.

He was born in Moffat, Dumfriesshire, in September 1882, the oldest of four children. His father was a headmaster. Curiously, in a short biography he included in his booklet *Many Mansions*, published in 1943, Dowding made no reference to his roots. He simply starts by stating that, 'After an entirely undistinguished career at Winchester and . . . [the] Royal Military Academy, Woolwich' and proceeds to list his appointments over the following years till his retirement from the RAF in 1940. There's no obvious reason why he should ignore his origins, but it's in keeping with a man who was far from being the orthodox military man one might expect, particularly during this notoriously stuffy era.

When Dowding began his military career in 1900 there was, of course, no air force, so he was commissioned into the artillery. Flying, however, attracted him, and while serving in India the opportunity came his way to take lessons. In January 1914 he attended the military Central Flying School and when war broke out in the same year and the potential of aeroplanes for military use was appreciated, it was a natural progression for Dowding to sign up for the Royal Flying Corps. He was,

© Getty Images

Hugh Dowding

therefore, in at the beginning of the development of the plane in warfare and understood the relevant issues as well as anyone.

Dowding was undoubtedly a capable leader who rose to high position without the social position and connections that can so often provide the less talented with a leg up. In 1940, as Britain was threatened by invasion from Germany and the Nazis sought to dominate the skies over the United Kingdom, Prime Minister Winston Churchill insisted that Dowding, who was due to retire from his position as Commander-in-Chief of the RAF, stay on and lead the fighter defence of Britain. It was a role that was to end in a controversy that has echoed down to the present day. Why was Dowding, who is generally recognised as the man who masterminded the defeat of the Luftwaffe in the Battle of Britain, unceremoniously sacked in October 1940, at the very moment of the RAF's greatest triumph? It's an event that has puzzled historians ever since, but there are some clues to be found in unlikely places. Hugh Dowding had some strange beliefs, as it turned out.

In her autobiography *The Psychic Life of Muriel, The Lady Dowding*, published in 1980, Muriel Dowding, Hugh Dowding's second wife, was still grappling with issues that were swirling round her husband's sacking forty years before. She felt an obligation to defend him against rumours circulating that had been put forward to explain his sudden downfall. 'I would like to make one point absolutely clear,' Lady Dowding wrote. 'Contrary to the misapprehension of many people, Lord Dowding did not win the Battle of Britain through Spiritualism. He did not, in fact, begin to study the subject till three or four years after the Battle when he retired.' So had Dowding been mixed up with the occult at a key moment of Britain's struggle against Nazi Germany, or was it an interest that only arrived on the scene after he retired as Fighter Command's boss?

One fact to note is that even after he was forced out of Fighter Command, Dowding continued to carry out other duties, including representing, at Churchill's behest, British interests in the USA. Dowding did not formally retire till 1946, and during the period 1943 to 1946 he wrote several booklets on spiritualist and occult matters and appeared in the newspapers in connection with the subject of the supernatural. It was, however, his and his wife's contention that Dowding did not become interested in these matters till after the Battle of Britain was over. The question is, did his interest in occult matters intrude into his handling of the Battle of Britain? And secondly, does this explain why he was so abruptly sacked?

Hugh Dowding was clearly a decent man. His wife, Muriel, has argued that her husband became interested in Spiritualism because of the letters he received from wives and mothers whose sons were either reported as missing in action or killed. There was an understandable wish to have more news about the fate of their child or husband. In many cases, however, there was no more information available and the Air Ministry and Dowding had simply no further details to give. It was for this reason, Muriel Dowding would have us believe, that her husband turned to the world beyond, in order to give comfort to the bereaved and concerned.

In 1943 Dowding's first writing on the subject of Spiritualism, called *Many Mansions*, appeared. According to Muriel Dowding's account, it was the result of her husband's reading across a wide range of material over an eighteen-month period covering psychical research, mediumship, materialisation, spirit messages and survival after death. She was at pains to make clear that Dowding himself during this period had not been personally involved in investigating psychics or any aspect of the occult. In her autobiography, she states categorically that it was only after the publication of

Many Mansions that he was taken by a friend to a séance where he sat with a medium for the first time. It was a determined effort to separate Hugh Dowding's involvement with the occult from his role as the Battle of Britain victor.

It was a line which Dowding himself was at pains to stress. On page eight of *Many Mansions* he stated that, 'So far as I am aware I am completely non-psychic. I have never had any super-normal experience, and I have never attended a spiritualistic séance'. A note at the bottom of the page reinforces this claim. Here he stated, 'This statement was literally true at the time when this book was finished. Since then, however, I have made several friends who have received from the other side messages addressed to me'. Dowding wrote that the booklet was finished in January 1943. The copy possessed by the National Library of Scotland in Edinburgh is date stamped 22 December 1943. It would appear, therefore, that *Many Mansions* was printed some time during the late autumn of that year. Dowding, then, would have us believe that he was not in contact with psychics till after he completed his booklet in January 1943, but in time to add a footnote before it appeared no later than November 1943. A very short but convenient window allowing him to emphasise that his involvement in the occult was initially no more than a broad interest in the subject and that it was as a result of writing *Many Mansions* that he took a more hands-on approach to and interest in the supernatural.

Of course, it might be asked whether the timing of his involvement in the paranormal matters. And why would he lie, or set out to massage the truth? It mattered to both him and his wife in order to safeguard his reputation and to hide a possible explanation for his sacking.

Dowding's involvement in the paranormal was formidable. His second wife, Muriel Maxwell, was herself psychic and claimed in later life to have seen Dowding in visions she had had as a little girl. Dowding, she wrote, was the figure in khaki who had calmed her down after her nightmares and promised that they would marry. She did not, however, realise that Dowding was the man in her earlier visions till they met. And the supernatural played another part in the development of their relationship. Muriel's first husband, Max, a member of a Lancaster bomber crew, was posted missing in June 1944 and it was to obtain further information that she wrote to Dowding. There's no doubt that by this date Dowding was actively involved with spiritualist mediums and offered to arrange for Muriel to attend a séance. Dowding went too and their relationship developed from there. They both had a keen interest in the other side and were soon devoting a considerable amount of time in contacting the spirit world.

Very little was too odd for Dowding to take an interest in. So involved was he in the supernatural that in 1955 he was invited to lay the foundation stone of the British Spiritualist Association's new headquarters in London's Belgrave Square. By 1963 Dowding had become a prophet for the New Age. In *God's Magic*, published in that year, he wrote of his belief that the earth was about to undergo a dramatic change. 'I believe', he wrote, 'that in this new age now beginning – this Aquarian Age – the flame of knowledge and enlightenment will spread like wildfire'. He held these views for the best of reasons. He wanted to see the world become a better place, and, as a man who had been forced to oversee the deaths of many young men, he yearned for an end to war.

But his philosophy led him down many strange paths. He came to believe in the existence of UFOs and met up with George Adamski from the USA, who claimed that in California he had encountered alien entities on a number of occasions and been taken up in a spacecraft. On the back of these accounts Adamski toured the world giving lectures about his experience. Dowding described him as 'sincere'.

Dowding was even convinced that Muriel could get in touch with the spirit who was the guardian angel of mice by giving out a 'love ray' which provided a contact between human beings and the world above. The mice, consequently, would leave the house on request and it was unnecessary to put down poison. Muriel Dowding spent years of her life campaigning to prevent cruel treatment of animals, convinced that they could be communicated with in this way. When Dowding was made a Baron and elevated to the House of Lords he acted as her mouthpiece on this, what must have seemed to many a strange belief. Whether fair or not, it's hard not to come to the conclusion that Dowding's views and actions in the years after the Battle of Britain raised questions about his role during that campaign. That is why there was such emphasis, by Hugh and Muriel, on the date when they claimed he became interested in the occult.

There are those who believe that in October 1940, when he was dismissed from his post as Commander-in-Chief, Dowding was simply stabbed in the back by jealous rivals. A number of prominent individuals have been named as involved in a conspiracy to remove Dowding, including Lord Trenchard, Head of Bomber Command; Sir John Salmond, Marshal of the RAF; Sir Archibald Sinclair, the government's Secretary of State for Air; and W.S. Douglas, Air Vice-Marshal. But what reason would they have for sacking him? Dowding was due to retire in any case at the end of October 1940, by which time it was clear that the Battle of Britain had been won. It would seem only decent to allow Dowding the opportunity to retire gracefully and accept the congratulations of a grateful country. Instead, at a meeting called for 17 October 1940, shortly before his retirement date, an unsuspecting Dowding was subject to a barrage of criticism over Fighter Command's tactics during the Battle of Britain and, as a result, removed from his post shortly after.

On the face of it, the argument centred on Dowding's criticism of what was known as the Big Wing tactic. This strategy involved using enhanced wing formation of up to sixty fighters to intercept large formations of the Luftwaffe rather than continuing to use single squadrons as interceptors. Dowding was sceptical of the claims being made for Big Wing successes and made no secret of his doubts, even though the Big Wing formations were backed by powerful figures in the Air Ministry. The most authoritative recent commentator on tactics employed during the Battle of Britain, Squadron Leader Peter Brown, endorses Dowding's criticisms, but also suggests that leading figures in the Air Ministry resented the success of Fighter Command and Dowding's role in that success.

There may well be much truth in that assessment, but is that the whole story? Dowding was due to leave. Why not simply let him go? There's no doubt that an attempt was made to bury him, but was that simple ingratitude? In June 1943 Dowding became the first member of the RAF to be offered a barony. In 1946 he was asked to write an official account of the Battle of Britain, both of which suggest that there was by no means all-out hostility towards Hugh Dowding.

Perhaps, he was his own worst enemy and his interest, one might say obsession, with the occult began long before he went public. In *God's Magic*, published in 1946, Dowding made a startling assertion. He wrote that he firmly believed that Germany's rise to power before World War II was the result of her 'deliberate and conscience alliance with the powers of darkness'. Dowding also made it clear that he defined black magic as the 'misuse of spiritual power and worldly and selfish ends'. Clearly, Dowding was endorsing the view that Hitler's Germany had been using Satanic influence to achieve its ends. Had he thought so at the time? Naturally, he would never admit it, but he did firmly believe in the ability of the spirit world to act on this world. He argued that 'the veil between the two worlds will become thinner and thinner' and that to bring about a better world the lead role should be taken by those on the other side.

Was Dowding's belief in the role of the supernatural in everyday life one that was known to his colleagues at the time of the Battle of Britain? Did his view of Germany's Satanic force colour his attitude towards Britain's role in the Battle of Britain? At the very least, Dowding's assertion that he only began to take an interest in the supernatural after he stood down from Fighter Command is open to question, and his views may explain why his colleagues were in such a hurry to bury the man who had served them so well.

John Duncan

I've often wondered whether the paths of Hugh Dowding and John Duncan crossed. Although engaged in quite different careers they shared an interest in the paranormal and Duncan lived for a while in London. During his lifetime – he died in 1945 – John Duncan was one of Scotland's best-known artists. His reputation was such that four years before his death the National Gallery organised an exhibition of over a hundred of his paintings, a unique honour at that time for an artist during his lifetime. It's a mystery then why his reputation plummeted thereafter, only undergoing a revival in recent years. Did it have something to do with his fascination with the mysterious and occult? As with many things in life, interest in the supernatural has its ups and downs, and aspects of it go in and out of favour. Duncan's involvement with the Celtic twilight, the myths of the enchanted lands and a concept popular during his lifetime, perhaps faded during the 1940s and 1950s, though it certainly resonated once again following the impact of the New Age movement and its aftermath.

Duncan, born in Dundee in 1866, started his artistic career in what he came to regard as hack journalism, producing illustrations for local newspapers and magazines. He had trained at the Dundee School of Art where his obvious talent for drawing ensured that he found employment as soon as he left the world of education. Moving to London he spent three years as a book illustrator, but he was desperate to develop what he saw as his real creative abilities and travelled to Antwerp and Dusseldorf to learn painting techniques. He returned to Dundee in 1891.

Was his involvement with the enchanted world as seen through his paintings present from early in life? Or something he came to in later years? The evidence has been disputed, but some of his earliest works, etchings dating from the 1880s, suggest a fascination with the macabre. He included a depiction of the Devil both in 'Lucifera', produced in 1888, and in 'Faust and Mephistopheles' in 1892. In another, Duncan drew a headless horseman and a girl around whom a vulture hovers. The etching 'Lucifera' is a strange artistic work by anyone's standards, but surely suggests that even at this early period in his life Duncan's imagination was transfixed by the inhabitants of the unseen world. Certainly the work might make one wonder over the state of Duncan's imagination. It depicts a procession – a feature Duncan liked using – of animals lead by a pig, followed by a donkey, a goat, a lion, a tortoise with bear-like features, a camel, and taking up the rear, a dragon hauling a chariot. The pig carries Bacchus, the god of wine and revelry, on its back, while a naked girl rides the tortoise. The chariot is driven by the Devil and standing inside is a queen examining herself in a mirror held in her hand. It's not clear what Duncan meant to convey, although it's certainly full of symbolism, drawn from a variety of world mythologies. The tortoise is well known in Hindu tradition as one of the ten avatars or incarnations of the god Vishnu. He is known as Kurma. Bacchus was adopted by the Romans from the Greek god Dionysus. The goat is well known throughout European legend as a symbol of Satan, and the dragon as a motif for paganism. Overall, it is a disturbing image. But what is curious is that Duncan in his painting moved away from these scenes depicting the evil aspect of the other world to paintings that exhibited a sense of the beauty and the more wholesome influence of the enchanted world. He would only return to the theme of an evil presence at the very end of his life.

Had Duncan encountered entities that preyed on his imagination? Was he anxious to get away from the thought of such creatures? He did not admit it, but on the other hand, he certainly believed in nature spirits such as fairies. He told his daughter that he could hear them talking to him and claimed to have seen them on Iona, one of the islands of mystery in the Hebrides that he loved to visit and paint. And if fairies exist, is that also true of less pleasant beings?

Patrick Geddes, the same man who influenced Charles Rennie Mackintosh, had a major impact on Duncan's artistic life. Geddes, a man of many talents, had started a magazine, *The Evergreen*, which became the vehicle of the Celtic revival, an attempt through resurrecting the myths and legends of past eras to bring about a change of attitude in society. It represented a reaction to industrialisation, urbanisation and the rationality of science. The magazine lasted only a few years, from 1895 to 1897, and then Geddes, its driving force, moved on to other challenges. Its impact, however, was significant to artists and writers and, probably, more widely in reviving a sense of the importance of the unseen world. It provided a platform for John Duncan, who contributed many drawings and illustrations. It launched him on a career which would turn him into a famous artist.

One can get a feel for the direction of *The Evergreen* by its content. There were short stories titled 'Sant Efflam and King Arthur', 'The Snow-Sleep of Angus Ogue' and 'The Black Month' or, in other words, the month of the dead. John Duncan contributed a poem called 'The Sphinx', an indication of his interest in ancient Egypt, apart from his many artistic inclusions, full of mystic symbolism. The end piece of one issue pictures an Egyptian obelisk, reminiscent of Cleopatra's needle, decorated with symbols rather than hieroglyphs. These include: the Masonic symbol, the set square; the wavering rays of the sun god Ra; a thistle; a butterfly and a sword, among others. A pair of sphinx at either side of the column complete the picture. It's doubtful whether a coherent message was intended, but it conveys a sense of the mysterious and the other world, which was the main focus of those such as John Duncan involved in this movement. As *The Evergreen* put it, 'the Celticists listen alone to the elemental voices, or strengthen the surviving and renewing unity of Brython and Goidel'. The Brythons are better known as the 'Ancient Britons', and Goidel as the Gaelic culture of old. It was essentially an appeal to the past and all the myths and legends that it represented. John Duncan certainly took the theme to heart and it became the key feature of his painting for the next forty years. He saw it as his mission to demonstrate to the world that our everyday reality was not the whole story, that there existed other worlds which edged into our own, that the myths of the past were not meaningless tales, but had a relevance for the present.

Following a spell in Chicago in the United States, Duncan returned to Scotland and over a period of fifteen years produced some of his best known and most mystical works, 'The Riders of the Side' or 'Shee' in 1911, 'Tristan and Isolde' in 1912, 'St Bride' in 1913 and 'The Children of the Lir' in 1914. The focus of all these works was the myths and legends of the Celts. During this part of his life he paid frequent visits to Iona, where it is said he encountered fairies. His visions of the island as a mystic location had a profound influence on other artists. Samuel Peploe and Francis Cadell, well known as key members of the Scottish Colourists, a school of painting favoured by Donald Dewar among a host of the well known, followed in his footsteps. The natural, mystic beauty of Iona, thanks to Duncan, caught the popular imagination.

But what was the message John Duncan was trying to convey through his art? His best-known work, 'The Riders of the Sidhe', is an important indication of what he was seeking to achieve. The 'Sidhe' or 'Shee' are the fairies of Irish legend who live in a hill at New Grange beside the River Boyne. It is surmounted these days by a famous prehistoric monument, which was probably erected there because of the site's link to the mysterious worlds. The tales of the Sidhe are very old, but their connection to New Grange may have risen as the memory of those who had actually built there faded with the passage of time. By tradition, the Sidhe emerged from their underground world on the Eve of St John, 23 June, the period of the summer solstice which takes place between 21 and 24 of the month. It is the time when the Sidhe initiate those they have chosen or encountered from the human world into the enchanted lands, at a sacred location known only to them. In the painting, the riders on horseback and incidentally drawn as the human-looking fairies of the old tradition, each carry an object symbolising aspects of the ancient Celtic tradition. The leader holds the Tree of Life, a symbol of wisdom, while the next carries the Grail cup and another holds a crystal through which is revealed both the past and the future. The painting was the clearest statement by Duncan of his belief that the realm of the supernatural, represented here by the fairy figures, can at times interact with our own everyday reality.

But for reasons that are obscure, following this spate of mystic productions, Duncan abandoned straight depictions of Celtic myths, apart from one brief interlude, only to return to it at the end of his life with an artistic production which caused a profound shock when it was put on display. Some have blamed Duncan's apparent loss of interest in the phantom world on his marriage to Christine Allen in 1912. It seemed to come out of the blue as Duncan was middle-aged at this point, having passed forty-five, whereas his new bride was nineteen years younger. John appeared very much in love with Christine and they had two daughters together. He was shocked when in 1925, with no apparent warning, she left him and emigrated to South Africa. What was worse was the fact that Duncan had no idea where she had gone and only learnt by chance when a friend bumped into her nearly three years later.

It's probably no coincidence then that in 1925 Duncan produced what is seen as his last straightforward painting in the Celtic mythology series. Its theme is the famous legend of St Columba bidding farewell to the white horse, which is also the work's name. The horse in ancient tradition was viewed as a magical beast and worshipped as a totem by many of the ancient Celtic tribes. Its association with Columba is more evidence of the manner in which pagan beliefs drifted into the themes and myths that grew up around the early Christian missionaries. In this instance, an old white horse comes up to Columba and starts crying. His fellow monks try to pull it away, but Columba tells them to leave the animal alone as it knows what they do not, that Columba will shortly die. It's a famous incident and Duncan's work is, again, a powerful affirmation of the influence of Celtic myth.

However, for the next twenty years till his death, John Duncan devoted his artistic effort on religious work, creating beautiful altarpieces and stained-glass windows for a range of churches. When he eventually returned to the supernatural, the theme he adopted shocked those who saw it and continues to disturb spectators to this day. The painting is called 'The Fomors, Or the Powers of Evil Abroad in the World'. It depicts a range of images, some grotesque and animal-like, moving forward in a group that includes human figures. At the centre of the picture a white shrouded individual rides on the back of a white horse – the spirit of death. In Celtic tradition, the Fomorians were a cruel, violent, misshapen race representing the powers of evil. They were warlike and terrorised the other tribes of Ireland, constantly attempting to conquer and rule over them. The thrust of the work couldn't be clearer.

Duncan displayed this work in 1939 as world war loomed, so it may have been intended as a comment on the evil forces that were being unleashed. There were many, especially with a mystical inclination, who saw in the Nazis a reflection of the less pleasant elements that inhabited the unseen world. John Duncan was in that sense a visionary, aware of the enchanted lands and that, as on earth, the force for good was counteracted by the force for evil.

'The Fomors' was Duncan's last mystical painting. It's said that he was shocked by the negative reaction to it. To some it was simply unpleasant and in sharp contrast to the Celtic themes he had portrayed in his previous works. Duncan, however, may have realised that he had revealed more about his inner view of the supernatural than he intended, and had finally decided that enough was enough.

Donald Dewar

It's well known now that Donald Dewar had a passion for art, although the public only became aware of it after his death. At time of writing, there is surprisingly no full-length biography of Donald Dewar, Scotland's first First Minister, a man so popular he was dubbed by the media as the 'father of the nation'. When a book does appear in due course, as I'm sure it will, it should make interesting reading. Dewar was certainly an enigmatic figure. A man obsessed with the location and structure of Scotland's new Parliament to a degree that puzzled friend and foe alike. What made him so determined to place the Parliament building in Edinburgh, in a location that seemed at first glance to many the most unsuitable of sites? And what led to the design of the building, a configuration that struck others as downright weird?

Donald Dewar was born in 1937 to middle-class parents. His father was a Glasgow consultant and Donald was sent to a private school in the Borders at an early age. From there he entered Glasgow Academy before studying Law and History at Glasgow University. Donald Dewar had a lifelong interest in politics, and in the era he grew up in, the Labour party presented the only choice in the west coast for those with no attachment to the Conservatives. From an early age, Donald demonstrated a formidable talent for debating and public speaking, so it was no surprise when he was chosen, against strong local competition, to fight the Aberdeen South seat for

Labour. His victory in the 1966 election on the coat-tails of Harold Wilson's popularity was no slight achievement, as it was the first time that the seat had been wrested from the Tories. He was only twenty-nine and a long career in politics beckoned. Unfortunately, however, in a swing to Edward Heath in the 1970 election, the constituency returned to its Conservative roots and Donald was forced back into law, becoming a reporter to the children's panel system, which had been recently set up. In 1978 though, he made a dramatic return to the political scene with a famous victory at the Garscadden by-election in Glasgow, a result which dramatically halted the then rolling and seemingly unstoppable Scottish National Party bandwagon in its tracks.

Donald Dewar, to both friends and the wider public, came across as an austere figure. He seemed little interested in wealth or possessions. The flat he lived in in Cleveden Street, Glasgow, was described by friends as being sparsely furnished. The carpets were threadbare. Paint was peeling off the walls. It lacked central heating and his television set was of such an ancient vintage that it didn't even use a remote control. On one occasion when he was due to fly abroad on a diplomatic mission he had to borrow a suitcase from a friend as he didn't have one of his own. He drove about in an ageing and battered car and seemed to have no interest in acquiring a newer model. As far as material possessions went, he appeared to live the life of a hermit.

There was general astonishment, therefore, when on Donald's untimely death in 2000, his will revealed him to have been a millionaire. He owned at least three properties, two of these were flats in the same street in the up-market area of Kelvinside in Glasgow. The one he had lived in was described as a 'fabulous ground floor conversion' and the other, slightly smaller overall, still boasted four bedrooms. They were valued at offers over £189,000 and £149,000, respectively. In addition, he owned a property in Stirling which he had bought from his aunt's estate on her death, but which, as he never made any use of it, remained unoccupied and empty. There was also a sizeable collection of paintings, the Scottish Colourist school in particular, and his library of antiquarian books. Many of the items he gathered are now on display at the Donald Dewar Room in the Scottish Parliament complex. It took conservationists two years to tidy up the collection of 1,800 objects.

There's certainly no criticism intended of a man for acquiring wealth. As has been pointed out, Donald inherited some of his art collection from his father, who was himself a man of means. Nor is it intended to suggest that he was being hypocritical. By all accounts, he was a kind and decent man who generated considerable affection among colleagues. He undoubtedly cared deeply about Scotland and its people. But what we see publicly is not necessarily the whole man, and it is this private aspect that helps to explain Donald's fixation on siting the new Parliament of Scotland at one location in particular.

Another characteristic of Donald Dewar, made much of by his associates, was his attachment to Glasgow. He was, as has been noted, not only born there, but spent most of his education at secondary and higher level in his native city. He won a great triumph there in the 1978 by-election and, in addition, had worked in the city as a solicitor. By all accounts, he enjoyed Glasgow's culture and lifestyle. Colleagues describe his life as being rooted there. It is said that his spirits visibly lifted when he approached Glasgow if he had been away for any length of time. According to former Prime Minister Gordon Brown, to Donald Dewar the city was home. So why was he so determined then to site the new Scottish Parliament in Edinburgh? It is, at the very least, curious.

Certainly, at one level, it could be argued that Edinburgh was the obvious choice. The old Scottish Parliament that had voted itself out of existence some 300 years earlier had sat in the capital, and as the capital Edinburgh had a strong claim to be the location for the new legislature. But on the other hand, Scotland was a very different country from that of 1707 when the parliaments of England and Scotland had been united. For one thing, Glasgow hardly existed at that time. But by the 1990s over half the population of the country lived either within or in close commuting distance of the city. Arguably, in terms of wealth, industry and finance, Glasgow had a stronger claim in the new democratic Scotland to having the new Parliament located somewhere within its urban sprawl. It would be a symbolic break with the past and a pointer to a new future.

But Donald Dewar, in spite of his attachment to Glasgow, had no interest in the city as a location for the new Parliament. He wanted it to be in Edinburgh and had his mind set on one spot in particular. And, as he was regarded as a key figure in the creation of a devolved Parliament, he was in a prime position to see his wishes carried through. It was Donald Dewar, who as Secretary of State for Scotland, having been appointed to the position by Prime Minister Tony Blair following Labour's 1997 election victory, had been the guiding hand in devising the legislation and steering it through the UK parliament. He had been elected as Member of the Scottish Parliament for the Anniesland Constituency and then to the position of the first ever First Minister. It was at this time, riding a wave of popularity, that he earned the title 'father of the nation'. He had the authority and, it seems, the legal right to decide the vexed question of where the new Parliament building should be housed. Some, especially in the Scottish National Party, advised him to consult with the newly elected body of MSPs, but Donald was determined to press on.

Glasgow having been ruled out, the choice lay between the Old Royal High School building at Calton Hill, a site in Leith and a location at Holyrood. Many assumed that the Royal High School would be chosen, as Holyrood was seen as a non-starter raising too many logistical issues, whilst not many favoured Leith. There was general astonishment, therefore, when on 8 January 1998 the Holyrood site was given the green light. After Donald's death one former cabinet minister expressed his continuing puzzlement over Donald Dewar's abandonment of the Royal High School as a location. It's a decision that continues to bemuse even though the furore over the huge cost of Holyrood's construction has, over the passage of time, somewhat died down.

Donald Dewar chose Holyrood for reasons that can only come under the heading 'mystic'. There can be no other explanation as there was no sensible reason for choosing the location otherwise. One factor only stands out in its favour. The site was steeped in history, and in supernatural association. On a visit to it in April 1998, he enthusiastically extolled the historic significance of the location. He said in a press release:

> The start of the archaeological work is another milestone on the road to establishing Scotland's Parliament. It is Scottish Office policy to conduct appropriate archaeological and historical work in advance of new building and the site, *at the heart of so much Scottish history*, offers an unrivalled opportunity – before the site is developed – to examine the reality of that history in detail. Historic Scotland has already examined documents and maps to establish as far as possible the history of the site. [my italics]

The history associated with this spot meant everything to Donald Dewar. Many of his colleagues have reported his fascination with Scotland's past, his enthusiasm for the tales of Sir Walter Scott among others, his knowledge of the era of William Wallace and Robert the Bruce. Holyrood, in the shadow of Arthur's Seat, that most mystical of hills, and as the location of King David I's supernatural confrontation with a stag, among other strange incidents connected to the area, was steeped in both history and the mysterious. It's hard to believe that Donald, described as an expert on Scotland's history by those who knew him intimately, was unaware of the legends linked to the spot. I'd suggest that he revelled in its associations, and the thought that the new Scottish Parliament would reside in this mystic site.

Interested observers, however, experienced a further shock when the architect and the design for the new building were unveiled. Enrico Miralles Moya was not a name that immediately rang any bells – in Scotland at any rate – and the new plans for the building looked quite simply strange. Enrico Miralles was a Spanish architect, but a project on the scale of the Parliament building looked, on the face of it, at a different level from that which he had previously dealt with. The publication *Who was Who* lists his commissions as including, prior to 1998, the archery range in Barcelona for the Olympic Games and the Huesca Sports Hall. There were others, but overall it seemed a sparse record, although Miralles had won architectural prizes for his work. More important perhaps was the fact that Donald Dewar seemed to hit it off with the forty-three-year-old designer. A panel had been set up to consider potential architects and designs. It was chaired by Donald who was also, by all accounts, the driving force, which is understandable given his overall role. There was general astonishment, however, when Enrico Miralles was selected and also by the proposed design. Puzzlement over the whole affair of the Parliament building turned to bafflement which became disbelief, as the cost of the project rose from £40 million to £400 million and beyond. Unfortunately, the untimely death of Enrico Miralles at only forty-five in July 2000, followed by the unexpected death of Donald Dewar in October 2000, have left many unanswered questions over why things turned out as they did.

I'd suggest, however, certainly as far as Donald Dewar was concerned, mysticism lay at the heart of it and that included the design of the building. Most found it puzzling. Why was it surmounted by what appeared to be a succession of upturned boats? However, I doubt if Donald would have gone along with a design so mundane. Like many, I've looked at the structure from various spots, including Arthur's Seat. I'm inclined to go along with the suggestion that it resembles the all-seeing eye of the ancient Egyptian god Horus, but a motif that has been used through the centuries in various guises including, as is well known, the US one-dollar bill. At first sight such an idea might appear outlandish. However, as a symbol, the Eye of Horus was intended to bring wisdom and enlightenment to those who possessed it. I'm sure that Donald Dewar was aware of its significance and would have taken pleasure in the knowledge that this motif had been built into his great achievement of the Scottish Parliament, intended to benefit those who occupied it.

In November 2011, Justice Minister Kenny MacAskill MSP was pictured practising Tai Chi with a group of enthusiasts outside the entrance to the Scottish Parliament building. It made good press. But the the exercise more aptly reflected the strange forces involved with the establishment of our Parliament than those involved in this demonstration of Eastern mysticism might have guessed, or even been remotely aware of.

7

Full Circle

Does the land of Scotland possess a mystical aura? An atmosphere of other worldliness which has influenced successive generations from the mists of times past to the present? Or is it something in the genes that produces a people for whom the supernatural is not something intangible, but another form of reality as significant as that which we live in every day? The origins of the Scots are disputed. There's a long tradition, as recounted in the history of our land compiled in the fifteenth-century book the *Scotichronicon*, that the people who came here thousands of years ago were descendants of the ancient Egyptians, and that the country was named after one of their princesses, called Scotus.

Whatever the truth of that legend the mystery surrounding the creation of Scotland is in keeping with a country that can boast a constant flow of supernatural events. From the first sighting of the Loch Ness Monster in the sixth century, through the miraculous appearance of the cross of St Andrew in the sky before the battle of Athelstaneford in 832 AD, the rising fear that Satan's army was invading the kingdom in the sixteenth century, to the claimed sightings of entities from distant planets in the twentieth. Scotland can point to haunted houses, castles and every conceivable building in between in their thousands. From St Mungo to the present day this land has produced a never-ending stream of seers, mediums and psychics, not to forget those who possess an apparent ability to break the known laws of physics by supernatural means. Wherever we turn, the paranormal, openly or subtly, has had a far greater influence on our history and on the people who have made history than has been usually recognised.

Even rulers are not immune. While James VI saw the supernatural in the evil form of witchcraft as a threat, David I, monarch from 1124, viewed his encounter as a wonderful and mystical experience. It's a well-documented incident, as well, and one that has already been briefly mentioned in this book. King David was hunting in the shadow of Edinburgh's Arthur's Seat, woodland in those days, when he was confronted by a white stag with prominent antlers. The stag knocked David to the ground and wounded him in the thigh. The deer would have killed David if a crucifix had not miraculously appeared in his hands. Faced by this Christian symbol the stag broke off its attack and disappeared. That night, David experienced a vision that, having been saved by divine intervention, he should by way of repayment build an abbey. David was so sure that he had experienced a mystical event that he had a monastery erected where the stag had appeared. It was built near the site where the present Parliament building now stands. In this way the Holyrood area was firmly fixed at an early date as a mystic location, an association that, as explained in chapter six, was to reverberate down the centuries.

Alexander Thomson

However, the supernatural has not only influenced the location of buildings, but the form they have taken too. This can be

Alexander 'Greek' Thompson's St Vincent Street church

seen in the work of Alexander Thomson, the Stirlingshire-born architect who lived from 1817 to 1875. He is internationally famous for his work, much of which he carried out in Glasgow. On the surface, Thomson was a committed Presbyterian who held a position as Elder in his church and who insisted on prayers every evening at home. But his architecture told a different story. A fascination with the style, decoration and symbolism of the ancient world which earned him the nickname 'Greek' Thomson. Why would a man apparently devoted to a Christian god, the supreme being, shape his buildings, including religious houses, to resemble the temples of pagan idolatry? It's a mystery, but Thomson was surely aware that in the Victorian era in which he lived anything less than outward commitment to religious conformity could bring professional suicide. He lived, in truth, a double life.

His architectural commissions are imbued with a mysticism that has impressed successive generations. Although it's the Greek connection that has stuck, Thomson was, in fact, equally if not more impressed by the way in which the ancient Egyptians had created an atmosphere of mystery in their buildings. He expressed the view that Christians had the Egyptians to thank for persuading people of the immortality of the soul, an early suggestion of the link between the religion of ancient Egypt and the formation of Christianity, and a theme which has re-emerged in recent years. To take one small instance, the ankh of ancient Egypt can by its shape be argued to be the forerunner of the Christian cross. It's seen as evidence of the input of ancient religious practice into the 'new' religion. Thomson's insight that there may have been an historical association could explain why he was so willing to adopt the style and colours of Egyptian temples into the Christian churches he created in Scotland.

The church he designed at Glasgow's St Vincent Street in

1859 is generally recognised as the building that typifies his mystical style with its use of light to create an aura of other worldliness. He based the layout on the temples of ancient Egypt, with their rows of windows, strategically placed to separate the outside from the interior whilst illuminating that which was sacred inside. Here and at the now demolished Queen's Park Church, he made use of a variety of motifs from mythological traditions from around the world, including Hinduism. The interiors of the church at St Vincent Street are coloured red and blue, the traditional decoration of ancient Greek temples, but also of ancient Egypt, where the colour blue, that of the sky, was viewed as sacred.

That Thomson was influenced by the mysticism of paganism is clear by his strange observation as a Christian that 'Stonehenge is more scientifically constructed than York Minster'. The mystical aura connected with pre-Christian beliefs clearly had a profound influence on Thomson, much of whose work, unfortunately, has been demolished.

Wendy Wood

There's certainly no pattern over who is influenced by the paranormal or who experiences a supernatural event. An encounter with the other world may have a greater effect on some more than others. And a ruler, or a person who has a brilliant reputation in one profession or other, may simply because of their fame be able to make more of it on the public stage than a lesser known person. David I and his battle with the mystic stag stand out in that context. Wendy Wood, on the other hand, may not be a name on everyone's lips, but in her time during the 1950s and 1960s she was well known though seen, perhaps, as a bit of an eccentric.

I remember her as the remarkable woman who I used to see speaking during the 1960s at the Mound in Edinburgh. She was a Scottish nationalist when it wasn't fashionable to be so and spoke with tremendous fervour about Scotland becoming an independent nation again. I can still picture her standing on her 'soap box', ruddy-faced, with a feather mounted on her tartan cap, determined but with a sense of humour, dealing expertly with doubters and hecklers. But Wendy too had experienced some remarkable paranormal incidents that she documented in several books. Perhaps the most dramatic was her encounter at the mountain pass of Lairig Ghru, which she described in *The Secret of Spey*, one of the earliest accounts of the mysterious phantom known as the Big Grey Man. This legendary entity is a strange figure believed by some to be Scotland's Yeti or Big Foot. It's purported by some to be a monstrous being, part ape, part human which hides itself within the mountainous regions at remote spots, only occasionally venturing out. To others the Big Grey Man is simply an evil spirit inhabiting the realms of the unknown. Sometimes it appears as a solid being. At others, it seems like a spirit of the dead rather than a flesh-and-blood animal. No one is quite sure what to make of the contradictory tales surrounding its existence. Wendy Wood's encounter reveals the bizarre nature of this phenomenon.

As Wendy told it, she was walking through the mountains on a dull day with a scattering of snow lying on the ground. Having travelled as far as she wished and with light fading, she decided it was time to turn back. At that moment she heard a voice, very loudly, in her ear. It sounded as if someone was speaking to her, though she couldn't make out the words and thought it might be in Gaelic. However when she looked round there was no one there. Mystified, Wendy attempted to identify a possible source for the noise. Had it been the echo of an animal's cry? Just at that moment the voice sounded again, but this time it appeared to be coming from beneath her feet. Alone, and as she herself admitted, disturbed by the incident, she nonetheless spent some time searching for the person who she believed had been shouting to her. However, there was no one to be found, and suddenly feeling very lonely, Wendy decided that it might be a good idea to get away from that spot.

As she set off she was startled to hear the sound of footsteps following behind. She tried to reason that it must be a weird echo of her own, but realised that these footfalls, which suggested something of a massive stature, in no way matched her stride. Now quite frightened, she hurried down from the hill till at last she reached a farm cottage. The barking of a dog seemed to bring the chase, if that's what it was, to an end. Wendy claimed that she was unaware of the Big Grey Man tradition and only learned of it when she talked about the strange event she had experienced.

Did the mystery tradition of Scotland encourage Wendy Wood in her nationalist campaign? She is certainly now regarded as a bit of a romantic. In fact, Wendy wasn't born in Scotland, but in the English county of Kent. Having listened to her on several occasions, I believe she was inspired in her fight for an independent Scotland by the mystic aura she associated with this land. The books she wrote, including *Tales of the Western Isles* in 1952 and *Legends of the Borders* in 1973 suggest that she saw in a separate Scotland an opportunity to resurrect the ancient Celtic land of myth. I'd hazard a guess that she would find the Scottish National Party of today engaged in a very different crusade. However, her campaigning in the period after World War II undoubtedly helped to keep the flame of nationalism alive.

Highland Seers

I don't think it would be an exaggeration to suggest that Scotland has produced more mystics and psychics per head of the population than any other country on Earth. There have been so many Highland seers that whole books have documented their predictions and prophecies, and that is not including those of the best known, the Brahan Seer. In fact, there has been a long line of Highland mystics from Celtic times to the present whose influence in their local communities has been immense. These 'witches' and 'warlocks' were consulted on everything, from the best time to conceive a baby to how to ward off the evil eye. However, they seem to be best remembered, if collected tales are anything to go by, for their prediction of individual fate.

In the 1920s, Sarah Gunn, who lived near the town of Wick, earned a reputation as a woman to whom impending dreadful acts were revealed, which generally discouraged people from approaching her. Best known is her prophecy that within her lifetime many bodies would be washed up along the Caithness coast, a prediction that came true, as following the outbreak of war in 1939 a large number of ships on convoy duty were sunk in the surrounding seas. The dead sailors were carried by the tide to the nearby shore, exactly as the seer had foreseen. Sarah's prediction, it has to be admitted, gives a flavour of the doom-laden prophecies traditionally linked to the northern mystics.

In areas of the Highlands, the entities of the enchanted realms weren't simply creatures that you might encounter by chance. They were part and parcel of everyday life. Most families of note either had their own mystic who they consulted regularly, or were linked to a supernatural being. The Shaw family of Rothiemurchus, near present-day Aviemore, had an elf as a servant, although he was popularly known as the Goblin of Doune. The Grant family, meanwhile, claimed two house fairies, or brownies, as a part of their retinue. To have such a creature on your side was considered a badge of honour, the medieval equivalent of a status symbol. In practical terms, the support of the supernatural would give you the edge over your enemies, a thread that continues to the present day. The drive to uncover forbidden knowledge and put one's self at an advantage is a key reason why, even in our technology-obsessed times, people dabble in magic rituals, attempting to contact those beings who live in worlds outside our own.

The feeling that the mystics of Scotland, particularly of the Highlands, were more in tune with the other worlds than those of elsewhere influenced organisations beyond Scotland's borders. Samuel Mathers, the founder in the 1890s of the best-known and most important society of magic (in its mystical sense), The Golden Dawn, adopted the traditional Highland name MacGregor as his middle name to cement his image as a man of mystery and as a true inquirer into arcane knowledge. Similarly, the better-known Aleister Crowley, the Great Beast, who liked to dress in traditional Highland garb and whose name is a byword for the modern form of black magic, changed his name from Alick to Aleister to achieve the same effect.

Robert Ogilvie Crombie (ROC Crombie)

However, one of Scotland's most remarkable seers was a Lowlander, the mystic Robert Ogilvie Crombie, better known as ROC, a resident of Edinburgh. Crombie made the remarkable claim that in 1966 in Edinburgh's Botanic

Gardens he encountered a satyr, a creature with the head and torso of a man, but the body of a goat with shaggy legs and cloven feet. A few months later as he was walking towards Princes Street the god Pan appeared to him and engaged him in conversation.

ROC claimed that he regularly saw nature spirits of all kinds. Was it an over vivid imagination? Maybe, but his visions had a significant impact, as Crombie became friendly with Eileen and Peter Caddy, and in the 1960s they set up the Findhorn Foundation near the village of the same name. Now regarded as one of the key spiritual centres of the world, it has had an astonishing influence on the New Age and post-New Age generations. It was ROC who, through his conversation with the nature spirits – fairies, elves and gnomes – learned that the spot at Findhorn would be the best location for their enterprise. And the rest, as they say, is history.

Crombie was following in a long tradition of mystics who are directed by the supernatural to a particular location. It's suggested that this is why Rosslyn became such an important centre, and it's true that St Mungo was active in the area. There's a well named after him in nearby Penicuik, although he can't be connected directly with the site of the present-day chapel. The impact on world consciousness of this elaborately decorated church needs no re-telling, as it has featured in books, films and numerous documentaries. Do we Scots take our role as the planet's hot spot of mysticism in our stride? I would say a definite 'yes' to that. There's nowhere else with such an extensive and current tradition of the supernatural, but Scotland seems to accept it all without even blinking. The industrial heritage of Glasgow and the administrative heartland that is Edinburgh somehow seem to sit easily with a deep channel of mysticism.

Maybe it simply doesn't register at a conscious level. There's been much speculation over the reason why the Knights Templar fled to Scotland after their expulsion from France in 1307 and their excommunication by Pope Clement V. Suggestions have been from the mundane – that, as the whole land of Scotland had itself been excommunicated, the Pope's writ did not apply there and so, strictly speaking, it was a safe haven – to the mystical – that for the Templars Scotland was their spiritual home. Whatever the truth, there can be little doubt that this organisation had a huge impact on Scottish society in its encouragement of secret ritual and stimulation of a sense of the mysterious. It's yet another factor to be added to the cooking pot of Scottish mysticism.

Gary Gray

But what can we learn from the psychics of today? Is there anything that the famous from the past, in the spirit world, would wish to tell us? I discussed the matter with top Scottish medium Gary Gray. I have known Gary since 1998 when I first met him for an article I was writing for my 'X-Files' column in the Glasgow *Evening Times*. Even by then Gary, who was in his twenties, had gained a tremendous amount of experience in contacting those who have 'passed over'. Like many gifted mediums, he was aware of his ability to see spirit people from an early age. At nine years old he encountered an elderly silver-haired ghost one night. He did not recognise the person at the time, but later picked him out from old photographs as an uncle who had died some years before. At an even earlier age Gary's parents were aware of voices coming from his bedroom when there was no one there. Objects would move in his presence and, more dramatically, when Gary, aged four, caught his arm in an electric wringer it miraculously switched itself off – otherwise his arm would have been badly crushed. Gary has a number of spirit helpers, individuals on the other side who communicate and help him in his work. There's a wee lad called George, about eight years old, who follows Gary about everywhere, and Gary's twin brother Stephen, who died in 2007.

Gary and I have been involved in several psychic investigations. Our strange experiences at Greyfriars Kirk in Edinburgh, site of intense poltergeist activity, I have described in my previous book, *Edinburgh After Dark*. However, Gary's presence at the site of the Battle of Sheriffmuir near Stirling had a more practical purpose. The line of the new and controversial power-line running from Beauly near Inverness to the Borders would cross close to, and some argue across, the site of this famous battle, which took place during the 1715 Jacobite uprising. How would the spirits of those who were killed during this encounter feel about this disrespectful treatment of a site where so much blood had been shed? According to Gary, any work at the site would greatly upset the spirit world. As he informed a reporter from the *Sunday Express* who listened as Gary tuned in to the other side, 'It is as if you are being watched. There are human remains in there and the builders will come across them. I think they will discover either four bodies or four lots of bodies.' Gary certainly confirmed that any work on the site would have to be sensitively carried out.

In 2011, at my suggestion, Gary took on an equally dramatic project to solve a long-standing mystery, an attempt to discover more information about the origin and purpose of seventeen miniature coffins with carved figures inside discovered on Edinburgh's Arthur's Seat in the nineteenth century. These objects are now on display at the National Museum of Scotland in Edinburgh and have even featured in an Ian Rankin novel. The suspicion has always been that the coffins, found concealed in a hole by a group of schoolboys in 1836, had been used for some black magic purpose. Gary, having with the permission of the National Museum surveyed the coffins, followed this by a visit to Arthur's Seat. Here he confirmed that the coffins had been connected to occult practices of some kind. He told the *Sun* newspaper reporter Matt Bendoris, 'These coffins were definitely involved with witchcraft. Their intention was to cause harm.' Gary also identified an area beside Dunsapie Loch where the dark arts had been practised. It certainly all seemed to fit.

Having been involved with Gary on these and other projects and having heard him communicate with the spirit world, I had no doubt that he could provide a fresh window into the paranormal experiences of those I'd written about in *Famous Scots and the Supernatural*. However, would they be willing to communicate with me, albeit through Gary? However, Gary confirmed that contacting the spirits of the famous would be no different than getting in touch with anyone else, if they were willing to communicate with him.

Having established that fact I then had to decide who we could choose. Those I had written about all offered fascinating possibilities. Had Conan Doyle found fairies on the other side? What did Mary Queen of Scots have to say about the murder of her husband, Lord Darnley? Had John Logie Baird met up with Thomas Edison in the spirit world? Many thoughts whirled round in my head. In the end I suggested to Gary that we focus on individuals from three different eras with separate interests: King Arthur, Hugh Miller and Donald Dewar. In Arthur's case, I was hoping to learn if he had a strong connection to Scotland. Hugh Miller had been fascinated by the paranormal. Had this driven him to suicide? And why had Donald Dewar insisted on the location of the

Parliament building at Holyrood? I didn't know whether we would learn anything. It was down to Gary and the spirit world, but I thought it was an experiment worth following through. I was delighted that Gary agreed to attempt it.

In the end we visited locations with a direct connection to the three individuals we had selected. Suicide is always a painful and dramatic event, and equally so for those left behind. So why did Hugh Miller end his life in this terrible way? With Gary I visited Hugh's grave at the Grange Cemetery in Edinburgh in May 2012. The red granite plaque on the wall is a modest reminder of a once famous man and, surprisingly, lists none of his achievements. Perhaps he wanted it this way. A burning sun and clear blue sky formed a sharp contrast to the dark and depressive manner in which Miller had brought his own life to an end. But Gary sensed his presence immediately. From the spirit world it seemed that Hugh was pleased that he was being contacted. Gary heard a word which he repeated to me as 'Libya'. It took me a few minutes to realise that what he was, in fact, getting was 'Lydia' the name of Hugh's wife. Hugh kept apologising to Lydia for what he had done, explaining to Gary that he had put the gun to his chest because he simply couldn't take any more. Gary also picked up the voice of Lydia reassuring Hugh that he 'wasn't weak'. Clearly, the manner of his passing was still preying on the dead scientist's mind.

Interestingly, Gary had the feeling that Hugh Miller wasn't alone when he died. As has been noted, the manner of his death was a puzzle. But could he have been murdered? It seems unlikely, but if his suicide was assisted that appears unlikely too. It was interesting that Gary sensed that Hugh had been used in his lifetime to contacting the spirit world. Much more, it appeared, than people at the time realised. Hugh repeated several times to Gary that he was now with

Lydia and his family and was content in his environment. He was anxious, however, that his legacy to the world would not be forgotten. I'm sure that he can rest easy on that score.

I've always been intrigued by the alleged connection between Edinburgh and King Arthur, so our next stop was Arthur's Seat, situated at the heart of the capital. Would Gary find evidence there to substantiate a historic link to the legendary monarch? The result was less clear than at Hugh Miller's graveside, which was to be expected given that we were at a site where human activity had taken place over a period of several thousand years. As we sat beside Dunsapie Loch looking across the Firth of Forth, Gary did make contact with an individual from around the time of Arthur. Gary was able to confirm that the king had been active in the area, that he was a real person and was Scottish. He also heard the name 'Marguerite'. This may have had no connection with Arthur, although there is a 'Margante' associated with him, an alternative name for Morgan le fey, or Morgan the fairy, the half-sister, in some accounts, of Arthur and possessed of magical powers. He also heard the name 'Juan', which has a direct link with Arthurian legends, as he appears in the traditional tales as the King of Castile, a region of modern day Spain. Gary described Arthur's Seat as a 'time bomb of energy', which is an appropriate description. I'm sure that many people walking its slopes can sense the energy pulsating through the rocks beneath. It would be an apt spot to be linked with a person of mystical stature like Arthur. So perhaps the association can be explained in that way. People felt it was a place that should have a connection with him, and so over time they became as one.

Finally, we visited the Scottish Parliament building. This was the one I particularly anticipated, as I wished to find out if we could learn more about the reasons why it was

223

erected here. Donald Dewar's determination to build at this spot continues to baffle and has never been satisfactorily explained. In a sense, it wasn't surprising that Donald's ghost, phantom, spirit – however one chooses to call it – is present here. According to Gary, he loves this location and is proud of the part he played in creating it. All he wanted to do, he explained to Gary, was to give the people of Scotland a voice. I'm no psychic, but I have to admit that as we walked around this strangely constructed building you could sense Donald's presence in every beam and girder. Repeating the words of Donald Dewar from the spirit world, Gary told me, 'This area is where democracy started. It had to be here.' As I took in this comment from the 'father of the nation' I couldn't help thinking of David I and his confrontation hundreds of years before with that mysterious stag, and the King's immediate realisation that here, at this spot, there existed a powerful mystical presence. In a way then history has repeated itself and even in our modern age we cannot escape the influence of the unseen world.

Concluding Thoughts
and Remarks

If there is one thing that stands out for me in writing *Famous Scots and the Supernatural* it is that the paranormal is always with us. It may take different shapes and forms, and society at different eras has a different focus, but the world beyond the veil, as the nineteenth-century spiritualists so poetically described it, is as much a part of our world as the sun or the moon.

It's strange to note that the astonishing advance in science and technology has not dispelled a belief in the paranormal. Far from it. The supernatural is as much a part of contemporary society as the latest computer device, perhaps even more so as it has deeper roots. As society reaches for the stars, claims about the supernatural seem to expand in response as if the world needs both a science and a counter-science to balance everything out, a sort of global yin and yang. I would cite the example of author David Icke, whose claims that leading figures of the world may be shape-shifting alien reptiles, have resulted not in ridicule but worldwide fame. Mr Icke's books may lie at the extreme edge of the paranormal, the fringe element as it were, but they are in keeping with a society which maintains a deep interest in all aspects of the supernatural. More traditional beliefs in phantoms of the dead and the ability of some to communicate with spirit forms are as strong as ever. People can be on their computer one minute and visiting a spiritualist medium the next. The belief in the world beyond has not been defeated by science. It's clear that to many people the paranormal lies outside science and that ghosts, fairies and poltergeists might well exist, even if science says that it is simply not possible.

Well-known people are no more immune from the influence of the supernatural than anyone else. Of course, individuals in sensitive positions might wish to keep the lid on their interest in this subject for perfectly understandable reasons. And that fear of ridicule runs throughout society. At various times police officers, airline pilots, salesmen, to name a few occupations from the many witnesses who have reported their experiences with the supernatural to me, have all requested anonymity when I have written about their encounters. They have no wish to see their careers affected by admitting to an involvement in an unexplained event. Others are reluctant to put their heads above the block for the simple reason that they worry that their neighbours might laugh at them. Who can forget the jeering that followed US President Jimmy Carter when he admitted to seeing a UFO? Admittedly, that was back in the 1970s, but I suspect that if the same thing were to happen today we might see the same result.

I think that there is ambivalence about the paranormal which reflects not the fact that it appears not provable in a scientific sense, but that it is disturbing to our everyday reality. And I would suspect that it is the potentially disturbing aspect of it that gets people worked up when a politician, to take one prominent occupation, appears to be involved in the occult. When these two worlds collide – everyday reality and the paranormal – nerves start to jangle. We all like certainty, and the supernatural upsets it. Certainly, there are those who *want* to believe in fairies, but equally there are those who would refuse to believe in them even if one came and sat on their knee.

Of course, the idea of international conspiracies by those involved in the black arts and other mystic contacts is nothing new. In past centuries, organisations spread across several continents, such as the Illuminati, the Knights Templar and the Freemasons, among others, and have all been suspected of taking part in rituals involving aspects of the supernatural and using their contacts with other worlds to influence leading figures. All that has changed in the twenty-first century is that the alleged conspiracies have not simply gone global but quite literally universal, with alien entities being branded the culprits. Hidden among us, disguised as humans, they are the ones, some suggest, who are pulling the strings.

If it isn't aliens who are the culprits then it might be vampires. They have a long history easily stretching back in Scotland to the thirteenth century when there were many reports of individuals who had risen from the grave to feast on the blood of the living. In recent years they have made a considerable comeback and, as I write, the release of the film *Abraham Lincoln: Vampire Slayer* sums up the current fascination with the blood-sucking genre and also displays how the paranormal linked to the famous makes an ever bigger impact. No one, of course, is suggesting that a movie along these lines is other than fantasy, but it certainly reflects not only a fascination with the supernatural, but a continuing theme that in some shape or form those at the top of society have a greater interest and involvement in the world of the occult than they admit to in public. I've lost count of the number of times that I've heard suspicions voiced about the involvement of leading figures in witchcraft rituals. Personally,

I've never seen any evidence to back these claims up. But I've no doubt that, even as I write, someone somewhere will be suggesting there's a cover up involving aliens or Satanists.

There certainly are Satanists, as it's become a recognised religious sect and, as scientists tell us, given the number of potential earths in the universe, there may well be aliens too. But whether either is involved in a conspiracy to do us down is open to debate. Accepting the supernatural doesn't mean that we have to believe in every claim made on its behalf. I have to say that most of those I have come across in Scotland involved in the paranormal, either as mediums or witnesses, have no particular axe to grind on the subject. Mediums seem to take it all in their stride as a part of life, and more often than not witnesses are either simply puzzled or intrigued by their experience with no wish to take the matter any further.

The feeling that something exists alongside us but can't be seen by most of us has encouraged a continual flow of mediums. Scotland has produced in recent years many who have earned considerable reputations. I've mentioned Gordon Smith, who has authored several books on the subject, and Gary Gray. In the 1990s, Rita Davidson, known professionally as Darlinda, another Glasgow-based medium, also made a considerable impact, her services being used by several well-known figures, including actors and performers. Darlinda was followed by another Glasgow-based medium, Ruth Urquart, Ruth the Truth, who spent several years as a psychic 'agony aunt' for *Chat* magazine, the *News of the World* and the Glasgow *Evening Times*. I worked with Ruth on a number of radio programmes dealing with the paranormal. It all indicates that the supernatural in contemporary life far from being pushed back by science has been attracting even more attention.

An indication of this is the continuing campaign to overturn the medium Helen Duncan's conviction. Readers will recall that in 1944 Helen was convicted of breaking section four of the 1735 Witchcraft Act at London's Old Bailey Court following her vision at a public séance of one of the sailors on the sinking ship *H.M.S. Barham,* a disaster the British government was trying to keep the lid on. There's little doubt that this was a politically motivated prosecution carried out to keep Helen quiet. Seventy years on it still rankles with spiritualists. A petition to the Scottish Parliament in 2008 was turned down and the Criminal Cases Review Commission declined to take it on board, as, reportedly, it was felt not to be in the public interest to reopen it. Campaigners, however, have refused to give up and are currently seeking a judicial review.

Physical mediums, those who produce spirit forms using the substance called ectoplasm, as Helen Duncan did, are rare. I have never seen it, though I did see many spirit faces produced by Ray Tod, an Edinburgh-based medium. Ray, a small, unkempt individual living in straitened circumstances, was no one's idea of a psychic. However, he was generous of his time and never asked for a penny for the many demonstrations he gave me, and others, of his astonishing ability. Ray would go into a trance, for want of a better word, and then face after face of a deceased spirit form would appear as clearly as if you were viewing it on a television screen. Hard to believe unless you'd seen it with your own eyes, but there were many witnesses to this bizarre phenomenon. Ray had no famous clientele to my knowledge, nor did he seek any. According to what he told me, all he wanted to do was prove to anyone interested in the reality of the afterlife. In one sense Ray, who is now deceased, was typical of most of Scotland's mediums who are giving demonstrations of their ability at a grassroots level, at public meetings, or on a one-to-one basis without any thought of earning money.

There are, of course, two intriguing questions which have
no doubt arisen in everyone's minds as they have read through
Famous Scots and the Supernatural. Why were these well-known
figures influenced by the supernatural? And to what extent
did it affect their daily lives? In some instances it is perhaps a
bit more obvious than others. James VI, the Earl of Bothwell
and Mary Queen of Scots lived during an era in which there
was widespread belief in the existence of the Devil and that he
recruited individuals, the witches who became his followers.
On top of that the consultation of psychics, though they did
not go under that name, was a regular occurrence even if the
practice, in theory, was frowned on. It's hard to argue against
the notion that during this period at any rate the issue of the
supernatural played a major part in certain events that took
place, although that does not mean that other factors weren't at
play. Individuals even during this era could separate everyday
reality from the paranormal and questioned whether things
that happened weren't simply a natural occurrence rather
than a supernatural incident. James VI refused to believe at
first that the storms raised against his ship as described in
chapter two were anything other than the accepted forces of
nature. He had to be persuaded otherwise. What there was,
however, was a sense stronger than today that the other world
was close to ours and that the forces of evil that existed in that
world were out to undermine our own.

This was a departure from earlier periods. William Wallace
and Robert the Bruce lived at a time when no one doubted
the existence of the supernatural and there was an assumption
that the spirit carried on after death. There was also a belief
in the existence of evil beings, vampires for one. However,
the idea of an organised army of evildoers hadn't yet arrived.
The leaders of the people wanted to have the forces of the
supernatural on their side and went to some effort to rally

these supernatural troops. The portrayal of William Wallace as a mystic, now relegated to the footnotes of history, is a classic example of the importance to the medieval mind of having as your leader a man with a foot in both worlds.

Supposedly, as the belief in witchcraft melted away so did the whole idea of the supernatural. The lives of key figures from Scottish history show that this was far from being the case. Sir Walter Scott, a man with a worldwide reputation and judged to be Scotland's greatest writer, was completely fascinated by the paranormal. He not only included many supernatural incidents in his novels, but collected books on witchcraft and had a bizarre collection of strange objects with an occult connection. This aspect of Sir Walter has been downplayed, as has been Robert Burns' preoccupation with the paranormal as shown, among many other incidents, in his writing 'Tam o' Shanter', probably the most famous supernatural poem in literature. However, in place of Burns the mystic, we get Burns the political activist, even though there's no evidence that his politics was more important to him than his interest in the paranormal.

Admittedly, with writers and artists it might be hard to separate the product of their imaginations from a genuine belief in the supernatural. On the other hand, if it didn't mean much to them, why write about it in the first place? However, in the case of both Burns and Sir Walter Scott, there's more than enough evidence to suggest that they took the supernatural seriously, and it was because of that interest that they incorporated it into their fiction.

Sir Arthur Conan Doyle, however, was a complete opposite. A man who took the supernatural so seriously that he believed it would cheapen it by including it in his writing. For Sir Arthur his most famous creation, Sherlock Holmes, was fantasy. The spirit world, on the other hand, was reality. His campaign to prove that there was a world beyond reflected a growing resurgence in Spiritualism and the belief that through particular people – mediums – these phantom beings could be contacted. It can certainly be argued that Doyle helped to usher in the 'anything goes' syndrome, that any aspect of the supernatural no matter how ridiculous it may seem, the existence of fairies being a good example, is beyond the pale. If there is evidence for it, if a medium tells us that it is true, then it must be so no matter how bizarre it may appear. Lady Muriel Dowding, wife of Sir Hugh Dowding the architect of the Battle of Britain victory, was willing to believe that even mice have a guardian angel and that by contacting this spirit the animals could be persuaded to leave a house without the need for traps. Because his wife believed it, Sir High was willing to believe it.

There's no denying that for those who accept the reality of the supernatural its influence can take many forms. For the artist John Duncan it appeared in his paintings through his fascination for the ancient myths and belief in the existence of nature spirits that he reproduced in his best-known works. Charles Rennie Mackintosh expressed his mystical ideas through the designs incorporated into individual rooms and building projects where the influence of the male and female was balanced to produce, as he saw it, a more profound unity. It is this aspect, influence through design, which I suggest in part also explains Donald Dewar's support for the strange plan that became Scotland's new Parliament building at Holyrood. Following in the footsteps of Mackintosh, he appreciated the effect that a building can have on those who work in it through the aura it generates. Donald, I would argue, was very much aware of the mysticism linked to the Parliament site and believed in the beneficial effect of locating it there.

As Scotland heads towards a new phase in its history it's fascinating to note that in the building that represents the future, the mysticism that is so much a part of our country has not been forgotten and has found a fitting symbol.

Bibliography

Ardrey, Adam. *Finding Merlin*. Mainstream, 2007.

Alexander, Wendy, ed. *Donald Dewar*. Mainstream, 2005.

Bingham, Caroline. *Robert the Bruce*. Constable, 1998.

Blake, Fanny. *Essential Charles Rennie Macinktosh*. Lomond Books, 2005.

Brown, Peter. *Honour Restored*. Spellmount, 2005.

Bruck, Herman und Bruck, M.T. *The Life of Charles Piazzi Smyth*. Bristol Hilger, 1988.

Cairney, John. *The Quest for Charles Rennie Mackintosh*. Luath, 2007.

Cooke, Grace. *Plumed Serpent*. 1942.

Coren, Michael. *Conan Doyle*. Bloomsbury, 1995.

Crawford, Alan. *Charles Rennie Mackintosh*. Thames & Hudson, 2002.

Dixon-Kennedy, Mike. *Arthurian & Celtic Myths & Legends*. Sutton Publishing, 2004.

Dowding, Hugh. *Many Mansions*. Rider, 1943.

Dowding, Hugh. *God's Magic*. Spiritualist Association of Great Britain, 1963.

Dowding, Muriel. *The Psychic Life of Muriel, the Lady Dowding*. Quest, 1981.

Forster, Margaret. *The Rash Adventurer*. Secker & Warburg, 1973.

Gray, Affleck. *The Big Grey Man of Ben McDhui*. Lochar Publishing, 1988.

Gray, Affleck. *Legends of the Cairngorms*. Mainstream, 1987.

'Haig Papers'. National Library of Scotland.

Haig, Dorothy. *Douglas Haig: The Man I Knew*. 1936.

Halliday, Ron. *The A–Z of Paranormal Scotland*. Black & White Publishing, 2000.

Halliday, Ron. *Haunted Glasgow*. Fort Publishing, 2008.

Halliday, Ron. *Edinburgh After Dark*. Black & White Publishing, 2010.

Harris, J. *Douglas Haig and the First World War*. Cambridge University Press, 2008.

Hawken, Paul. *The Magic of Findhorn*. Souvenir Press, 1975.

Hogg, Patrick. *Robert Burns*. Mainstream, 2008.

Holder, Geoff. *The Jacobites and the Supernatural*. Stroud, 2010.

Hughes, Gillian. *James Hogg*. Edinburgh University Press, 2007.

Jarron, Matthew, ed. *The Artist & The Thinker*. University of Dundee: Museum Services, 2004.

Kamm, A. and Baird, M. *John Logie Baird*. NMS, 2002.

Keay, John & Julia, ed. *Encyclopaedia of Scotland*. HarperCollins, 1994.

Kelly, Stuart. *Scott-Land*. Polygon, 2010.

Lamont-Brown, Raymond. *John Brown*. Sutton, 2000.

Marquand, David. *Ramsay MacDonald*. Cape, 1977.

Maxwell-Stuart, P.G. *Satan's Conspiracy*. Tuckwell Press, 2001.

McArthur, Tom and Waddell, Peter. *Vision Warrior*. Orkney Press, 1990.

McNamee, Colm. *Robert Bruce*. Birlinn, 2006.

Mead, Gary. *The Good Soldier: The Biography of Douglas Haig.* Atlantic Books, 2008.

Miller, Karl. *The Electric Shepherd.* Faber and Faber, 2003.

Miller, Russell. *Adventures of Arthur Conan Doyle.* Pimlico, 2009.

Parsons, Coleman. *Witchcraft and Demonology in Scott's Fiction.* 1964.

Robertson, R. Macdonald. *Selected Highland Folktales.* Oliver & Boyd, 1961.

Shandler, Nina. *The Strange Case of Hellish Nell.* Da Capo Press, 2006.

Smith, Catherine. *The Stars of Robert Burns.* DOICA, 2008.

Smith, Gordon. *Spirit Messenger.* Hay House, 2004.

Stewart, Jules. *Albert: A Life.* I.B.Tauris, 2012.

Sutherland, Elizabeth. *Ravens and Black Rain.* Constable, 1985.

Taylor, Michael. *Hugh Miller.* NMS, 2007.

Various. *Donald Dewar: A book of Tribute.* Stationery Office, 2000.

Wood, Wendy. *The Secret of Spey.* R. Grant, 1930.